**More praise for Dr. Susan Jeffers
and *Dare to Connect***

"A loving, spiritual book that facilitates compassion rather than blame, inner-strength power rather than victim power."
Warren Farrell, Ph.D.
Author of *Why Men Are the Way They Are*

"Susan Jeffers writes with both love and no-nonsense common sense—a rare combination. She speaks directly and points the way to magical relationships."
Wayne W. Dyer
Author of *Your Erroneous Zones*

"A book of truth from a woman who truly walks the path herself—the path towards wholeness and love. Susan's new book comes straight from the heart and is very helpful for everyone, especially for those feeling isolated and lonely."
Margaret Paul, Ph.D.
Author of *Healing Your Aloneness*

DARE TO CONNECT

REACHING OUT IN ROMANCE, FRIENDSHIP, AND THE WORKPLACE

Susan Jeffers, Ph.D.

FAWCETT COLUMBINE

NEW YORK

A Fawcett Columbine Book
Published by Ballantine Books

Copyright © 1992 by Susan Jeffers

All rights reserved under International and Pan-American Copyright Conventions. Published in the United States by Ballantine Books, a division of Random House, Inc., New York, and simultaneously in Canada by Random House of Canada Limited, Toronto.

Library of Congress Catalog Card Number: 93-90028
ISBN: 0-449-90543-8

Cover photo by Lisa Law

Manufactured in the United States of America

First Ballantine Books Paperback Edition: September 1993
10 9 8 7 6 5 4 3 2 1

To my children,

GERRY AND LESLIE GERSHMAN

On their journey toward wholeness, they have taught me so much about loyalty, love, and life. My respect, admiration, and love are enormous.

And, as always . . .

To the "miracle" of my husband,

MARK SHELMERDINE

His support, generosity, wisdom, and love never cease to astound me. I am truly blessed.

Acknowledgments

As I write these acknowledgments, I am reminded of the tremendous amount of support, caring, and love that exists in my life. I am truly grateful.

Joëlle Delbourgo, my editor, who with great wisdom showed me how to "pull a diamond out of the rough." Her guidance gives me great confidence. **Thank you, Joëlle.**

Dominick Abel, my agent, who gently reminds me when I need to hear it, that "it's all happening perfectly!" His friendship is so welcome in my life. **Thank you, Dominick.**

Mandi Robbins, my assistant and friend, who made my life flow so that I could write this book with peace of mind. Her loyalty and gentleness are welcome gifts to this world. **Thank you, Mandi.**

The men and women who generously shared their feelings with me about love, friendship, and the workplace. They have truly made a difference in your life and mine by sharing who they are. **Thank you, beautiful people.**

The men and women who let me know that my work has touched their lives. Their feedback so greatly touches mine. **Thank you, beautiful people.**

My wonderful friends, who support the very best that I can be. With such great friends, life is a banquet. **Thank you, dear friends.**

Gerry Gershman and Leslie Gershman, my children, who are always a wondrous vehicle for my own personal growth. **Thank you, Gerry and Leslie.**

Guy and Alice Shelmerdine, my stepchildren, who have lovingly expanded my world. I respect and admire who they are. **Thank you, Guy and Alice.**

Joyce Shelmerdine, my mother-in-law, who has welcomed me into her heart. Her curiosity and enthusiasm are infectious. **Thank you, Joyce.**

Marcia Fleshel, my sister, with whom I share a bond of love and light that grows deeper every day. **Thank you, Marcia.**

Jack Fleshel, my brother-in-law, whose smile and caring light up my life. **Thank you, Jack.**

Mark Shelmerdine, my incredible husband. His contribution to my life is felt so deeply within my being. **Thank you, my dearest Mark.**

and

Jeanne Gildenberg, my mother, who, while no longer here in body, is always with me in spirit. **Thank you, Mom. I miss you.**

Contents

DARE TO CONNECT

REACHING OUT IN ROMANCE, FRIENDSHIP, AND THE WORKPLACE

Introduction

Many times throughout our lives, we experience painful feelings of loneliness and isolation. It would seem that the natural thing to do at such times is simply to reach out and connect with those around us. But as we all know from personal experience, feelings of self-doubt too often make the act of reaching out very difficult, if not impossible. As a result, we remain isolated from the very thing that can ease our pain . . . **the warmth of the human heart.**

Dare to Connect was written to give you insights and tools to ease any feelings of loneliness and alienation you may have. It provides answers to general questions about connection, and, more specifically, in the areas of romance, friendship, and the workplace. I have been trained in the field of psychology and I have interacted with thousands of people in my role as author, workshop leader, public speaker, and talk-show therapist. As a result, I am fairly certain that many of your questions will be similar to the ones I am frequently asked by others. For example,

3

Why do I feel so nervous when walking into a room full of strangers?

How can I pick up the phone and make that sales call without feeling so anxious?

Why is it hardest to approach the person I'm most interested in meeting?

Why do I feel so lonely, even though I'm always surrounded by people?

How can I overcome my fear of rejection?

How can I make friends?

How do I read someone else's signals?

What do I do if someone misreads my signals?

What do men really want from women? (And vice versa.)

What are the new rules about approaching someone for a date?

Why can't I ask for help at work where I so often need it?

Why do I feel so alienated from my husband (or wife)?

The people who ask these questions represent a huge cross section of the population—men and women, single and married, young and old, rich and poor, atheists and "believers"—yet their problems with connection abound.

Some want to be married but are locked into devastating insecurity when it comes to approaching a possible partner; some tremble as they walk into a business meeting or approach a potential customer or face an important interview; some ache for friends with whom to share their sadness and joy, yet totally wall themselves in when the opportunity for sharing arises; some are married, but still feel painfully alone.

Feelings of self-doubt and alienation are certainly not foreign to me. There was a time when my lack of confidence created isolation in all areas of my life. The simple act of walking into a crowded room produced butterflies in my stomach, sweaty palms, and a pounding heart.

I often dealt with my lack of confidence in inappropriate ways, including self-deception. For example, my first job required that I attend many business functions on my own. My habit was to walk into a room, take a look around at all the people who seemed to be happily engaged in conversation, decide everyone was boring . . . and leave as quickly as possible. One day, the obvious question popped into my mind: "How do I know they're boring when I haven't even talked to them?"

It was then that I came face to face with the underlying truth behind my thoughts and actions: "What if I introduce myself to someone . . . and they aren't interested in knowing me?" Obviously it was me whom I considered boring . . . not them!

Thankfully, I can now walk confidently into a crowded room filled with unfamiliar faces. Over the years, I have made many discoveries that allow me to reach out comfortably to others no matter what the situation. I wrote *Dare to Connect* to share these discoveries with you.

You may be someone who is comfortable in one arena, but a quivering mass in another. For example, you may find it easy to connect in business and friendship, but not when it comes to romance. Or you may be at ease in social situations, but unable to break the competitive barrier at work so you and your colleagues can support each others' professional growth. Regardless of your situation, valuable tools in this book will help erase your self-doubt as you move forward to connect with others.

You may wonder how similar concepts and techniques can apply in such diverse situations. Strangely they do. It won't take you long to discover that tools that bolster your confidence in one area of your life can't help but improve all other areas as well. For example, Tim, a trial lawyer who attended one of my workshops on relationships, found that the tools he learned for approaching someone of the opposite sex also make facing the judge and jury much easier!

Part I, **The Heart of Connection**, explains why we so often feel like a "Nobody," and then points us in the direction of feeling like a "Somebody" once again.

Part II, **The Journey Inward to Connection**, explores why we harbor feelings of inadequacy and loneliness and how to eliminate them . . . thus allowing healthy connection to occur.

Part III, **The Journey Outward to Connection**, presents the basic techniques of connection and those specific to the areas of romance, friendship, and business. (Even if you don't feel you have a problem in one or more of these areas, read *all* the sections. The concepts and tools in one section reinforce those in the others sections.)

Part IV, **The Soul of Connection**, shows you how to participate in the world in a way that could keep you from ever feeling alienated again!

There are many exercises provided throughout the book. They are meant to be incorporated into your daily life so that self-destructive thoughts are replaced by a healthy way of seeing yourself and the world around you. If you put these exercises into practice, in time, connecting with other human beings will feel like an act of love rather than a scary and potentially humiliating experience!

I suggest that you read through the book once. Then go through it again and again until you "own" it. Underline, circle, write in the margins; most important, make the exercises come to life. People who report the greatest success use my teaching as a starting point and then actually incorporate the tools and concepts into their daily lives.

As they have taken on the responsibility of *practicing* how to feel more powerful and loving in their day-to-day interactions, their lives have changed dramatically. Some have left unhealthy relationships or found healthy ones; some have become more successful in their careers; some have found wonderful new friends; some are simply getting more enjoyment out of life now that their insecurity has been replaced by a greater sense of confidence and peace of mind.

As you begin using the tools throughout the book, remember to be patient with yourself. Learn at a comfortable pace, not expecting overnight miracles. You have probably already made the unfortunate discovery that changing negative thinking and behavior patterns doesn't happen overnight. Change requires constant practice and repetition. Don't dwell on setbacks when they occur (and they will!); rather, focus on every little sign of progress. When you hit a snag or a setback in your ability to connect with others, simply pick up the book again and find the section that addresses the difficulty. Positive feelings will reappear, and you can face the world once again.

If you find the voice of impatience creeping in, just keep repeating:

ONE STEP AT A TIME IS ENOUGH FOR ME.

You'll find yourself changing significantly in ways that will allow you to be with others in a more confident and loving way. Most important, **don't give up!** The quality of your life is at stake! You are too important to deprive yourself and others of the power and love you hold within. Sharing ourselves with others gives life meaning and purpose . . . and a feeling of fulfillment and inner peace.

Dare to Connect is not your usual how-to book. It introduces an element that is absent in many well-intentioned books of this nature. I'll let you discover it as you progress. Some ideas seem obvious when pointed out, but remain painfully elusive if we walk blindly through life, too often alone and too often afraid.

I believe you will be deeply moved and challenged by the book. One of my students told me at the conclusion of a workshop: **"It wasn't what I expected, but it was much more than I could have hoped for."** I hope *Dare to Connect* touches you in the same way.

THE HEART OF CONNECTION

1

There Are No Strangers

When I was in my twenties, I was friendly with a night-club singer who always closed his act with the words "The most important thing that I've learned in my travels around the world is that **there are no strangers, only friends I've never met.**" His fans obviously loved it because they always responded to his words with applause, smiles, and tears. Being young and skeptical, I thought it was pure corn and manipulation, but I couldn't deny that he had touched a chord.

When I was in my thirties, I attended an all-day workshop with seven thousand other people in New York City's Felt Forum. The workshop leader came out onto the stage to face this awesome crowd and, after his opening thank-you's, stated, **"I don't know your names, but I do know who you are."** I recognized it as another version of my night-club singer's message, but being a bit older and mellower, I was able to catch the germ of truth in the words. Yes, in many ways, we are all the same: we all experience feelings of fear, pain, joy, anger, jealousy, judgment, happiness, sadness, generosity, greed, and every other human emotion.

When I was in my forties, I began seeking answers to certain questions that kept coming up in my mind:

> If, in fact, there are no strangers, why do we often feel so separate from everyone around us? Why do we often feel so alone? Why do we often feel like outsiders looking in? If we are alike in so many ways, why do we often feel so inferior?

I ultimately discovered that part of the answer to these questions lies in the way we have been **trained** to see ourselves relative to other human beings. One of my favorite models of this training process comes from the author and teacher, Ram Dass.[1] He suggests that when we are born, we immediately go into **"Somebody Training"**; that is, we are taught by our parents and our society that what we are "supposed to" be in this world is a Somebody! They define a Somebody as a person who has achieved some measure of *external* success. As a result, our "Somebody-ness," or self-worth, is dependent on such factors as money, status, power, personality, looks, and intellectual excellence.

You might ask, "What's wrong with that? Isn't our quest to be a Somebody and achieve some measure of external success in the world the source of much of our motivation and drive?" The answer to that is, of course, YES! But when we allow these trappings to become a measure of our self-worth, we set ourselves up for an incredible amount of pain, and **instead of feeling like a Somebody, we end up feeling like a Nobody!**

There are several reasons for this:

1. Somebody Training emphasizes individual differ- ences and puts us in competition with everyone around us. Hence, we are always on a treadmill trying to keep up with or surpass everyone else . . . or we just give up when the competition seems too great.

2. When we strive to fill ourselves up with approval from people "out there," we twist the essence of who we really are and create a false picture we hope will bring us the acceptance we crave. And when we lose sight of who we truly are, we feel empty inside.

3. When we focus only on externals, such as looks, money, success, sex appeal (ours or theirs), we lose sight of our common humanity. We lose sight of the feelings that lie within us all, of those unseeable qualities that create a sense of bonding. And we remain alienated.

Our external cards of identity have been important from a very early age. Think back to when you were young. How often did you feel like a Somebody and how often like a Nobody? How often did you feel too fat, or too thin, or too dumb, or too tall, or too short, or too loud, or too quiet, or too pushy, or too shy, or too selfish, or too much of a pushover . . . or too whatever. In order to be a Somebody, there was always something to "fix."

Even if there was someone in your life who was ex- traordinarily supportive, I bet you felt like a Nobody a great deal of the time. I did. I remember feeling like a Nobody when I came home from school with a B on my report card, because my parents believed that Some- bodies always got A's. I remember feeling like a Nobody when the boy I had a crush on didn't invite me to the seventh-grade dance. I remember feeling like a Nobody when schoolmates sang, "I don't want her, you can have her. She's too fat for me."

I was taught by my parents and society that to be a Somebody, one had to be smart (without letting the boys know just how smart), pretty, popular, a cheerleader, and the lead in the high-school play. Of course there were variations, but all of the other young girls in my class were programmed in a similar way. Naturally, the boys had their own special brand of Somebody Training; they were supposed to be athletic, tall, handsome, and drive flashy cars.

It didn't stop there. We were also programmed about how to be a Somebody when we grew up. The girls were expected to find a successful husband (which meant a rich and handsome professional), have a couple of kids, and be beautiful and adorable all of the time. The boys were expected to marry an attractive woman, get ahead in the workplace, and be the protector of the household.

It is true that times have changed since the Fifties in terms of social roles and expectations, but **nothing much has changed in terms of our Somebody Training.** We are still measured by our external achievements. No matter how evolved and supportive our parents may have been, no matter how much they built us up and tried to make us feel great about ourselves, it is virtually impossible for us to escape the framework of success set down by our society.

To see how this may have worked within your family unit, you might want to take the time to sit in a quiet place and write down your answers to the following questions:

Who did my parents consider to be a Somebody and what made them so in their eyes?

Who do I, today, consider to be a Somebody and why?

What do I think I have to "fix" within myself or achieve to make me a Somebody?

I suspect that your answers focus primarily on external rather than internal qualities that have to do with loving, caring, and sharing; that is, connection. You begin to see how much of our early conditioning needs to be reversed in order to topple our walls of isolation.

Incidentally, even those who fit all the external requirements of success seldom feel like Somebodies. Look at the self-destructive lives of Marilyn Monroe, Elvis Presley, and John Belushi. In the eyes of the world, they were Somebodies, but in the depths of their beings, they obviously felt as if they were Nobodies.

Author and counselor John Bradshaw sums it up when he says that because of our conditioning, we all live with a feeling of **"toxic shame"** (whether we are successful or not). We experience it as the pervasive sense of being flawed and defective as human beings.[2] This is hardly a good place from which to form connections in any area of our lives!

Equally devastating to our ability to connect is the way Somebody Training fosters an atmosphere of judgment. He or she isn't rich enough, attractive enough, outgoing enough, generous enough, ambitious enough, kind enough, and so on . . . and we put them out of our hearts. We put them down in order to puff ourselves up, not realizing that in the long run hurting others in this way makes us feel even more of a Nobody than we felt before.

While it is important to look at our upbringing to determine what hurtful teachings need to be corrected, it is important that we don't blame our parents. "Why not?" you say. "Look what they did to us!" In the first place, blame is a powerless act. It creates a feeling of helplessness instead of trust in our own ability to create a healthy sense of self. Secondly, our parents probably did the best they could given their upbringings! Were they not also a product of Somebody Training? Isn't their behavior, no matter how distressing and inappropriate, the result of their own struggles against feelings of worthlessness as they made their way in the world?

Sadly, I realize that in the name of love I did many of the same kind of hurtful things to my children that my parents did to me. And I observe other caring parents also trying very hard to do what's "best" for their children. Unfortunately, in a Somebody Trained world, that usually means correcting, molding, shaping, changing, and so on, until what's left of the child is a master actor who may look like a Somebody, but who feels like a Nobody. And Mommy and Daddy sit there applauding their handiwork (or wondering where they went wrong), not realizing they've lost their *real* child and created a fake.

Schools seldom help. I remember seeing a bulletin board in the entryway of an elementary school on which all the students were ranked according to their grades. Imagine the effect on the children's self-esteem. If the child who was number one dropped to second place, he or she couldn't help but feel like a loser—after all, he or she was no longer "the best." But my heart went out most of all to the children at the bottom of the list. I wonder how many of them cried themselves to sleep every night at the prospect of facing that telling list the next morning.

It is amazing how psychologically numb our entire social

structure is to the feelings of children. Observe children with their teachers or parents in the local playground. It's a real eye-opener! The number of negative messages that the adults give to the children is staggering! And even as adults, everywhere we turn we are reminded of our imperfections. For example, advertisers in magazines and the media sell us **illusions** which we will never be able to achieve in life. The puzzling fact is that we put up with it!

What this all means is that if we are conditioned to focus only on the external packaging, whether it's someone else's or our own, separation and loneliness will inevitably prevail and we end up with a society of what's been called "empty suits." And on it will go forever . . . **UNLESS WE CHANGE THE TRAINING.** The question is: How do we go about doing that?

Part of the answer lies in acknowledging that, while there is nothing inherently wrong with wanting to improve the externals of our life per se, our sense of connection with ourselves and the people around us does not come from externals; rather it comes from learning how to find that place within us all where **WE ALWAYS FEEL LIKE A SOMEBODY** and where **WE PERCEIVE EVERYBODY ELSE AS A SOMEBODY,** thus completing the circle of connection. There is no competition, only compassion. There is no fear, only love. There is no hate, only caring. (Sounds like heaven, doesn't it?)

Those of you who are familiar with my previous work know that I am talking about the place called the Higher Self. From this transcendent place it is possible to break down the walls of separation and bring us into harmony with ourselves and each other. There is no question in my mind that . . .

It is in the Higher Self that we find
the heart of connection.

If you are uncomfortable with the mention of the Higher Self, thinking it might have something to do with religion or God, take note that I am referring only to the inner spiritual part of our being: the best of who we are . . . the part of us that is loving, compassionate, caring, giving, abundant, creative, intuitive and knows there is nothing to fear. So **whether you believe in God or not,** the model will work for you.

The Higher Self, in the way I am using the term, is familiar to **all** of us even though we may not have labelled it as such. We experience the Higher Self during those times when we realize that "we are all in it together." For example, when we attend an event that is raising money to feed the hungry, we feel part of the collective human heart. Or when we all pull together at a time of crisis, we rise above the level of our individual differences and we stop competing. For those brief moments in time, the externals of our life, which usually seem so important, now seem petty and unimportant as we touch a more noble place within.

Given that the Higher Self describes a place that exists within all of us, and given that the Higher Self is the place where we feel connected to the whole human race (including that attractive person across the room with whom we would love to have dinner!), the important question is: **HOW DO WE GET THERE FROM HERE IN OUR EVERYDAY LIVES?**

The answer is that we need to enter into a new kind of training. I suggest we call it **"EVERYBODY TRAIN-ING."** The exercises in this new kind of training are designed to give us the strength to make the transition from Somebody (which excludes others) to Everybody (which includes others).

A wonderful demonstration of this transition from Somebody to Everybody is provided by the Olympics. During the games we see our Somebody Training in action: the intense competition of individuals; separation created by "us against them"; the disappointment of losing; and the elation of winning. But when the games are over, a magical transformation happens. The athletes enter the arena for the grand finale, this time not as competitors, but as part of the human family. They have dropped their national flags—the flags that separate. Any sense of struggle, fear, anger, and upset that went on during the games seems to have dissolved. We are aware of the communion, camaraderie, joy, even bliss that radiates throughout the stadium and into our homes as we watch the spectacle on television. Our hearts swell and it is hard to hold back the tears at the vision of what life could look like if we were able to transcend to that level of connection—that level of Everybody-ness—in all that we do.

Few of us know how, which is why there is so much yearning and emptiness in our lives. Thus it is my purpose to help you see the world through the eyes of the Higher Self, enabling your alienation to lessen and the loving essence of who you are to emerge. The pathway to the Higher Self is through the lessons of our Everybody Training.

So let's begin with an Everybody Training truth about connection:

Connection is made easier when we approach other people with the primary purpose of making THEM feel better about themselves.

The key word in this formula is **THEM.** The reason most of us are so fearful of approaching others is that, whether we are consciously aware of it or not, **we usually approach people with the primary purpose of making US feel better about ourselves!** Our hesitation about approaching others comes from the awful possibility that, instead of feeling better about ourselves after we make the big move toward connection, we'll end up feeling like jerks!

"Not me," you say, "I'm just shy." Think about it! The basic reason we are timid about making contact—whether for business, friendship, or romance—is that:

> We fear rejection.
>
> We fear that we are not good enough.
>
> We fear that we have nothing to say.
>
> We fear making fools of ourselves.
>
> We fear being put down in some way.

When we are afraid, we are not focusing on the other person at all. We are only focusing on ourselves! Our internal voice is *not* saying, "Perhaps that person is lonely and would like someone to talk to," or "Perhaps there is a way that I could make that person feel really good about himself." No, it is saying, "Perhaps she'll think I'm coming on to her," or "I look really lousy tonight and he'll find me totally unattractive." **We are so worried about the way we appear to that other person, that we cannot "see" that he or she may be needing something from us . . . even if it's only the reassurance of a smile.**

So we remain on opposite sides of the room, and, once again, we pass up an opportunity to make a loving connection with another human being. Or we physically connect, but, because of our nervousness, never really *listen* to what the other person is saying or *feel* what the other person is feeling. Hence, in effect, there is no connection at all.

Please note that I am not telling you all this to make you feel bad about yourself! I have a very deep compassion about how lousy so many of us feel about ourselves. I know how much it hurts to feel small and insignificant. I know some of us have been taught, directly or indirectly, that no one really wants to hear what we have to say, or that we are stupid, or that we should be seen and not heard, or whatever. I know how paralyzing these feelings can be.

So why am I telling you all this? First, to show you that the Somebody Training question **"What am I going to get?"** laces all our interactions with the fear of not getting . . . and, ultimately, not getting enough. The Everybody Training question **"What am I going to give?"** introduces a sense of outflow and abundance. To be the "giver" rather than the "getter" therefore makes us feel more secure.

Some of you may be feeling "Wait a minute! I give and give and give and get nothing back in return." I am not suggesting that you be a doormat for the hurtful people in your life. On the contrary, we need to walk away from people who treat us unkindly. What I am suggesting is that when we begin to see connection as a **giving** to someone, we can feel more at peace in our attempts to connect with others . . . **whether we are rejected or not.**

Of course, rejection *never* feels good: It always touches the insecurity within us, no matter how much confidence we have gained. But it sure feels better when we are not needing something from the person who is rejecting us. That I can guarantee! Ultimately, we learn that when we approach someone lovingly and are treated unkindly, we are learning much about *their* insecurities. **Secure people don't treat other people unkindly, no matter what the situation.**

John Powell has made the observation that we must use things and love people.[3] However, when we are fearful, we are locked into the trap of *using* people instead of *loving* them. This applies equally in all areas of our lives. People become objects to provide us with something we need . . . they do not appear to be human beings just like you and me with their own insecurities and their own need to be loved.

You now see why Everybody Training teaches us to focus on the giving instead of the getting. As you continue reading, you will learn how to put this concept into practice. For now, simply be aware that our own insecurities make it hard to give. As an exercise, you might want to keep a log of your interactions with other people, setting up different sections of the log for romance, friendship, and business. Leave a space to answer the following questions about each:

Did I approach this person with the purpose of getting something from him (or her)? Or did I approach this person with the purpose of giving something to him (or her)? (Something = praise, a job, a compliment, a thank-you, a date, sex, a sale, a favor, or a pat on the back and so on.)

If I approached this person with the sole purpose of getting something from him (or her), how might I have turned my thinking around to include giving something?

In the beginning, it isn't necessary to do anything with your answer to these questions. **As you become more aware of your actions and intentions, you will automatically become more giving to others.**

Be patient with yourself. Becoming a giver may at first be very difficult and uncomfortable. It requires that we let go of a lot of prior training. As we walk into the freedom that human connection allows, we may have to return to our isolation a few times before we can muster enough courage to fully embrace that world out there with outstretched arms. But as we slowly begin to feel better about ourselves, something wonderful begins to happen. The numbness starts to disappear and feelings of empathy and caring come pouring in.

By acknowledging that every "stranger" in that crowded room would love to feel cared about and has often felt themselves to be a Nobody, just as we have, we are in harmony with them even before we ever say hello. When this happens, we begin to understand the truth behind the words "there are no strangers," and the world doesn't seem so lonely anymore.

THE JOURNEY INWARD
TO CONNECTION

2

Finding the Warmth

The first time I met Jonathan was at a party. Clearly he didn't have a problem with connection in the way most people envision it. He talked to many people and appeared to be having a wonderful time—laughing, touching, listening, and so on. One would think he knew all the secrets of successful connection, and on a surface level, he did. But, beneath the surface, there was another story to be told.

I next met up with Jonathan when I was invited to sit in on a men's self-help group. It was in the safety of this group, which he'd been attending for six months, that he was able to talk with great poignancy about his many fears and unrelenting loneliness. He said, with tears in his eyes, that he went to parties, met a lot of people, yet usually ended up going home alone. Something within him was not allowing any true connection to occur. His greatest fear was that he would be alone and lonely for the rest of his life.

Hence, despite his successful party techniques, Jonathan is no better off in terms of his ability to connect authentically than the wallflower in the corner who never has the courage to walk up to someone and say that first hello. Despite the differences in the way they handle their exterior worlds, both are internally experiencing similar kinds of alienation from themselves and others. Let's take a look at what goes on **within** that prevents successful connection from occurring.

Did you ever ask yourself *why* people reach out to connect with one another? Of course, there are the apparent reasons—to find a mate, to gain new clients, to make new friends, and so on. But if we looked a little deeper, we would see a complex web of human emotions that makes us reach out for other reasons. Some of these emotions form the basis of healthy connection and others of unhealthy connection. Using the model of Somebody Training versus Everybody Training, let's take a deeper look:

EVERYBODY TRAINING REASONS
FOR REACHING OUT

To share our warmth and caring and love; to participate within the human family; to make the world, in our own unique way, a better place for all of us.

versus

SOMEBODY TRAINING REASONS
FOR REACHING OUT

To "fix" something within ourselves—such as our low sense of self-esteem, our unhealthy dependency, and our loneliness.

The difference is dramatic. And the implications are even more so. It stands to reason that when we reach out so someone can "fix" us, the results can be disappointing at best and humiliating at worst. We are assured of failure, since . . .

No one can fix what's broken inside except ourselves.

We may find a temporary fix, but, as we all know, temporary fixes always wear off and we find ourselves right back where we started.

Let's take romance as an example (remembering that the same model applies to other areas of our life). Sometimes we dive into romantic relationships in order to mask our neediness. Because relationships based on neediness are only Band-Aids for an inner problem, they are never fulfilling for very long, if ever. Remember what happens to Band-Aids? When you put them on, they feel clean, healthy, and secure. In a very short time, they get sticky and dirty, and ultimately you have to take them off before your skin gets infected! My own story demonstrates this Band-Aid analogy beautifully.

I met my first husband on my first day of college, as my father's car pulled away from the dormitory. We were married within the year. At the time, I felt very lucky to have found my "prince" at such an early age. It would take me many years to realize that the prime motivation for my marriage was not love (even though he was a terrific person and I loved him as much as I was capable of loving anyone at the time); rather it was the act of a dependent, frightened, and lonely young woman trying to find solace in a substitute parent.

It would also take me many years to realize that, while my marriage allowed me to mask the intense loneliness and fear that constantly lurked beneath the surface, these painful feelings always managed to seep out "sideways" in the form of anger, jealousy, judgment, unrealistic expectations, and feelings of abandonment and emptiness. Hardly a good basis for a healthy relationship! As I mentioned earlier, all the while I thought there was something wrong with *him* which was causing all my painful feelings and unloving behavior. I was too self-righteous (an obvious sign of insecurity) to notice that I had more than a few issues to work on within myself. How embarrassing!

When I ended my marriage after sixteen years, I felt that I would have no problem being on my own. After all, I was a big girl. Hence, I was not prepared for the anguish that I actually felt . . . anguish that came from feeling miserably lost and alone in the world. None of it made any sense to me then. On an objective level, I wasn't lost at all. I had diligently learned all the rules for being a Somebody in the world. I had two lovely children, a Ph.D. in psychology, a terrific job, a wonderful circle of friends, and no problem getting dates. My outer life was full, but my inner life remained unrelentingly empty. It was only then that I realized that my marriage had served as a Band-Aid. While my ex-husband and I remain very good friends today, our marriage had served to mask unresolved issues lurking since my childhood.

Looking back, I can now identify the feelings I was experiencing—loneliness, low self-esteem, emptiness, dependency, anger, and fear—as a form of **"Spiritual Separation,"** a lack of connection with the essence of who I truly was. The way I am using the term Spiritual Separation has nothing to do with religious belief or its absence. It has to do with a life lived without any connection to the Higher Self, that place **within** where all separateness disappears and a sense of wholeness appears.

Given our society's priorities, it is not surprising that one can go so many years without ever having faced the question "Who am I?" In an environment that conditions us to suppress our true selves and conform to the dictates of our parents, peers, religion, and society, there is little room for self-discovery and spiritual growth. Denied the knowledge of how to access this place of safety within, we constantly feel a yearning to return Home. We believe it must be our parental home that we are yearning for—the one we actually had when we were young (or the one we always longed to have!). We try desperately to create a new place of safety by attaching ourselves to someone else, but it never works for very long. Without our primal connection with our selves, true connection with others is impossible. And so the longing persists.

In my case, it was my divorce that set the wheels in motion for my Spiritual Separation to end and my Spiritual Connection—that is, my connection with myself—to begin. The truth about my loneliness, childlike dependence, and lack of self-esteem was finally out in the open and I could ignore it no longer. I had to acknowledge the fact that my prime motivation for latching on to other people was to keep the unrelenting emptiness at bay. Intuitively, I realized that the only way I could connect authentically, without an ulterior motive, was to acknowledge that the keys to hearth and home lie safely within my being . . . not in somebody else's. In order to feel this security, I had to "find myself"—whatever that meant!

I began to force myself to spend time alone, which is not so easy for a lonely and insecure person to do. In the beginning, my thoughts were filled with yearning, fear, and anger. I listened very carefully to hear the voice of the Higher Self that I knew lived somewhere inside of me, but which was now hidden beneath the many layers of conditioning. My pain reminded me how far I had traveled from the core of my very being.

Sometimes the solitude was terrifying; sometimes it was exhilarating. Sometimes I simply sat there clasping my abdomen, feeling that I would explode with the emptiness. Sometimes I was joyful about a new discovery I had made in my ability to enjoy life on my own. I cried a lot; I laughed a lot. I experienced a lot of fear; I experienced a lot of growth; because I didn't know who I was and what I liked to do, I began experimenting. I read. I went to workshops. I learned how to meditate. I traveled. I forced myself to eat alone in restaurants until I learned to love it. Slowly I began to find the unused parts of myself.

I also made changes in my outer world that went along with the changes I was beginning to feel inside. I let go of any friends who looked at life as an empty experience, and sought friends who saw life as a joyous and fulfilling adventure. I began to take more risks. I learned how to respect who I was and not to cave in to peer pressure. I lessened my need for approval from others, so it became easier to like myself. I learned that my life had value, and I participated fully in my job and my community.

All this growth was not an overnight process; rather it took place minute by minute . . . day by day . . . week by week . . . month by month . . . and year by year. And with each step, my life kept getting better . . . and better . . . and better. And then came the moment of triumph, when I realized that the yearning and fear and anger had been replaced by feelings of contentment, fulfillment, and love. I can now happily report that, while I don't feel connected with my center all of the time, this sense of wholeness permeates my being most of the time. And for that I feel truly blessed.

Twelve years after my divorce, having discovered how wonderfully a relationship works when emptiness has been replaced by a feeling of self-created fullness, I married again. The neediness that characterized my previous relationships has been replaced with a sense of genuine caring and sharing . . . and love. My experience has taught me that the three biggest barriers to authentic connection—low self-worth, dependency, and loneliness—have nothing to do with anyone "out there."

Our barriers to connection have only to do with our inner wounds that need to be self-healed and our inner fears that need to be self-calmed.

As we heal our inner world, everything "miraculously" gets healed in our outer world as well. Our lives become enriched with fulfilling jobs, supportive friends, and loving relationships. We begin to notice the beauty of all those people out there who would welcome our love. And in this wholesome space, loving connections can occur in all areas of our lives.

With that in mind, let's begin to look at some inner work that paves the way for successful connections to occur.

While it is true that we never break totally free from our earlier training, we can all learn to walk INWARD into a far more loving place.

3

I Want You to Like Me

Author and teacher Alan Cohen tells the following story: At the opening session of a human-relations workshop he attended, all of the participants were asked to write on a white gummed label something they wanted to tell about themselves to the others in the room. They were then to stick this little piece of paper on their foreheads and walk around the room reading the messages on everyone else's foreheads. An interesting way of breaking the ice, indeed! Most of the messages were of the "I love to travel," "I love racquetball," and "I just left a relationship" variety. But one message stood out in Cohen's mind as the one that said it all—the one that broke through all the **indirect** messages that were being presented—and that message was:

I WANT YOU TO LIKE ME.[1]

Metaphorically, we all wear an "I want you to like me" sticker on our foreheads. Whether we are conscious of it or not (and most of us are not), much of our behavior—good and bad—is simply part of an *Act* that we developed as children in the hope that it would earn us much-needed attention and/or approval. Our Act probably underwent some modification as the years went by, but the reason for the Act always remained the same—**WE WANT TO BE LIKED**. In fact . . .

We NEED to be liked.

John Powell presents us with a very poignant answer to the question "Why am I afraid to tell you who I really am?"

"I am afraid to tell you who I am, because, if I tell you who I am, you may not like who I am, and it's all that I have."[2]

A good clue as to why connection is so difficult! Implicit in this answer are the following truths we consciously or unconsciously hold about ourselves:

I want you to like me. But I don't like me. If you really knew me you wouldn't like me either. Therefore, I'll pretend to be different than I really am.

And to make matters worse, the person with whom we are playing this sad little deception is consciously or unconsciously saying to himself or herself,

I want you to like me. But I don't like me, and if you really knew me you wouldn't like me either. So, I'll pretend to be different than I really am.

And what we are left with are two people **trying** to connect, **wanting** to connect, **yearning** to connect, but who have no way of penetrating each other's masks. It doesn't matter whether these two people are sisters, brothers, parents, children, friends, co-workers, lovers, mates, "strangers" in the street, or some combination of the above. The masks are worn by all of us.

We don our masks very early in life. As helpless children, we are dependent on our parents for our physical and emotional survival. Therefore, we live with the terrifying thought that **"If I don't measure up, they might go away!"** Because of our terror, we begin hiding—and ultimately denying—the part of ourselves that could bring disapproval from our parents and, later, our teachers and peers. For example, if we are taught we must be generous, we disown the part of us that is greedy. If we are taught we can't be angry, we stifle the rage that is building within. If we are taught we must be strong, we hide our tears. If we are taught we must be physically attractive, we hide the "flaws" with makeup, deodorant, dyed hair, trendy clothes, cologne, shoe lifts, and so on. Consciously or unconsciously, we believe that no one could love us as we truly are. Eventually, we lose all sense of who we really are and our Act becomes our identity. What is left is a fearful robot who has long ago forgotten the answer to the question, "Who am I?"

When we are lost to ourselves, how can we possibly connect meaningfully with someone else?

This alienating pattern changes only when we begin the process of reconditioning ourselves to feel the enormous power and beauty that we truly possess!

You might be thinking, "It certainly sounds like some sort of vicious plot, that all of us grow up feeling inferior to some degree or another." It's really not. It has more to do with a society that truly believes that Somebody Training is a positive thing, a society that doesn't understand that its rules create an inability to love ourselves. Thankfully, we

can reverse the process and turn the self-hate into self-love.
I've provided some exercises to help you do just that. They
are meant to eradicate the false self and convince you that
you who you are is good enough. Only then can you allow
your authentic self to emerge.

I encourage you not only to read through these exercises,
but to take responsibility for incorporating them into your
daily life. Don't cheat yourself out of the joy of a life filled
with power and love that comes with improving the way
you feel about yourself. Remember . . . the exercises work
only if you do!

EVERYBODY TRAINING EXERCISES FOR LIKING OURSELVES[3]

STOP TRYING TO BE "PERFECT."   This is one
situation where "giving up" has to be the healthiest thing
you can do for yourselves. So breathe a sign of relief! Rest
easy as you stop trying to do the impossible. Understand
that the loveliest thing you can do for yourself is to **embrace the beauty of your humanness.**

A good start is to implant the following Everybody
Training thought in your mind by simply repeating it at
least ten times a day:

> **I am good enough exactly as I am . . . and who I am
> is a powerful and loving human being who is learn-
> ing and growing every step of the way.**

"Oh, come on, Susan! This hardly describes **me**!" On
the surface, it doesn't always describe me either! So what
does this statement really mean? It doesn't mean that there
aren't unhealthy patterns within us that we wouldn't like to

make healthier. It doesn't mean that we are always proud of the way we behave. It doesn't mean that we have learned everything we need to learn about becoming a more loving person. But it does mean that the essence of who we are is wonderful. It also means that every experience in our lives—the good *and* the bad—can enrich us in some way.

We learn that everyone's journey takes a different route. I might get there through years of being a driven perfectionist, you might get there through twenty-five years of a bad marriage, and your friend may get there through illness or alcohol. But from our different experiences, we ultimately can come to the deep understanding that we are all heading in the same direction . . . to the place of love within us all. In any case, the place and the person we are at this very moment is perfectly imperfect indeed!

An article by Linda Weltner entitled "The Miracle of Imperfection" points out that when we expect perfection in anyone, including ourselves, we are treating that person as if he or she is a machine.[4] (And even machines break down!) When we treat people as machines, we lose our human connection. I don't find it very satisfying going to lunch, to bed, to the movies, or to work with "machines." I'd rather be with human beings who sometimes make mistakes, get confused, feel insecure, get old, who reach out with their humanity and who touch the humanity inside of me.

It is through our humanness, not our perfection, that the poignant bonds of connection are finally formed.

BECOME AN EVERYBODY TRAINED PARENT TO YOURSELF. While our parents may or may not have been loving to us as we were growing up, it is important to keep remembering that we are all products of a Somebody Trained world. We have all been trained to feel "not good enough" about ourselves. Part of our inner work now is to provide ourselves with the unconditional loving approval unavailable during childhood.

Most of us do just the opposite: We go about our lives pulling ourselves down instead of building ourselves up. The negative internal voice I call the Chatterbox constantly reminds us of our "flaws," telling us we should be thinner, smarter, more organized, stronger, richer, prettier. It is clear that the Chatterbox must be silenced and replaced by a much more loving voice if we are to feel better about ourselves.

A very effective tool that provides this loving voice is the **guided visualization,** which is a closed-eye process. One of the several uses of guided visualizations is to allow your imagination to create circumstances in your life as you want them to be rather than as they may be at the present time. As the picture of your ideal life becomes clearer in your head, you are more likely to make the picture a reality. I've included a powerful visualization for connection, complete with an explanation and instructions, in the Appendix. It would be helpful for you to do this guided visualization before any social or business situation that makes you fearful. It will bolster your self-confidence enormously.

Another effective tool for replacing the Chatterbox is the **affirmation,** which is a form of positive "inner talk." Affirmations are strong positive statements that transmit the message to ourselves, "I'm really an OK person." Some examples of "loving-parent" affirmations that are meant to be repeated to yourself are as follows:

I am powerful and I am loving.
I have much to give to this world.
I am a person of worth.
I deserve love.
I am a capable person.
My life has meaning.
My life is unfolding perfectly.
There is plenty of time.

Note that **you do not have to believe these affir-mations for them to work!** The mere saying of them over and over again begins to reprogram the negative pictures you have of yourself. Set aside at least ten minutes a day to practice your affirmations. Use them every time you notice negative chatter going on in your head. There are many audiotapes available comprised totally of affirmations that you can listen to as you dress, lie in bed in the morning or evening, or drive to work. They help to obliterate the negativity and fill you with confidence. **Regular use** of affirmations can create remarkable changes in a person's life and I urge all of you to learn their proper use.[5]

To further remind you to be a loving parent to yourself, put signs all over your house, car, diary, and anywhere else you can see them that contain some version of "NO SELF-CRITICIZING ALLOWED." The aim is to catch yourself automatically when you begin putting yourself down. You can also enlist the help of your friends to point out to you how and when you unconsciously put yourself down. (It goes without saying that it is necessary to move away from the put-down artists you call friends who do the criticizing for you!)

Still another way we have of reprogramming ourselves and getting rid of our old critical Chatterbox is to

Remove those "I want you to like me" stickers from your forehead and, instead, place them where they truly will do the most good—on your mirror!

I'm speaking literally as well as figuratively! We actually need to *see* the message on the mirror so that our minds, which are usually so busy putting us down, will begin pulling us up. Most of the time when we look into the mirror, our Chatterbox sends us such messages as "Boy, I never noticed that wrinkle before," "My eyes sure look puffy," "My skin looks terrible." Every time you see something negative in the mirror, **switch to something positive.** This will help you learn to love the person looking back at you.

I know this isn't easy to do. Healer and teacher Louise Hay reports that the most difficult assignment she gives to her clients is to pick up a mirror and say to themselves, "I love you."[6] This exercise often brings up anger, sadness, and fear. She reports that as they continue practicing this exercise, most of them eventually get to the feelings of self-appreciation and self-caring that we all need in order to face the world with head held high and love in our hearts.

It is when we look into the mirror that we usually face our cruelest critic. Nobody can hurt us the way we hurt ourselves. It is important to remind ourselves constantly where our need for approval arises . . . and where it will finally end. We must be able to look into that mirror with confidence and approval and be able to say to ourselves, with total conviction,

Yes, I really like you. I appreciate the beauty of who you are. I would be proud to be your friend. I find you a strong and beautiful soul who makes my heart sing.

When we finally reach this point in our evolution, it doesn't matter whether someone else likes us or not and we can allow our authentic self to emerge . . . a first step in creating the bonds of connection.

FIGURE OUT YOUR ACT AND BEGIN DROP- PING IT.   As you can imagine, this is very scary in the beginning, since our sense of OK-ness is tied up with our Act. But when we finally peel away the layers of who we **are not,** and get to the core of who we **are,** we make a thrilling discovery:

WHO WE *TRULY* ARE IS VERY LOVABLE AND VERY POWERFUL.

It's a guarantee. How can I make that guarantee? Because as we get past all the Acts of who we are—the positive and the negative—and finally enter the place of our Higher Self, we touch the part of ourselves that is endowed with an inherent sense of power and love. It is also the place where "I am you and you are me." If, in our lives, any of us behaves in ways that are powerless and unloving, it's only because we've traveled so far from the essence of who we truly are.

As I explained earlier, when we allow our Higher Selves into our thinking, we can also embrace, instead of abhor, the "lower" part of who we are. That is, we accept that anger, greed, fear, and every other emotion that lives within us are just part of being human. With acceptance of all of who we are, we can then safely allow our masks to drop and tell the truth without fear of disapproval. (Can you see the bonds of connection beginning to form?) If someone disapproves, it doesn't matter. At this point, we will have finally gotten approval from the person we have been unsuccessfully trying to impress all these years . . . not Mother, not Father, not teacher, not the kids in the neighborhood . . . but ourselves.

To peel away the Acts that have removed us from our authentic selves, it helps to first identify our "I want you to like me" style or styles of behaving. Psychiatrist W. W. Broadbent identifies a few:

MAN'S-MAN STYLE (I'm absolutely fearless.)

SAINT STYLE (Aren't I sweet, smiling, loving, and accepting?)

WINDY STYLE (Aren't I wonderfully articulate?)

CHAMELEON STYLE (I'll be anything you want me to be.)

MORALIZER STYLE (I am virtuous and righteous and I always do what I "should" do . . . and so should you!)

FRIGHTENED-FAWN-IN-THE-FOREST STYLE (I am weak and need you to take care of me.)

MARTYR STYLE (Oh, all the things I've done for you and I get nothing in return.)

SUPER-SELF-SUFFICIENT STYLE (I don't need you. I don't need anyone.)

PLAYING-AUTHENTIC STYLE (Look how honest and forthright and authentic I am.)

TOILET-BOWL STYLE (Poor, poor me. The whole world is dumping on me!)

RED-CROSS-NURSE STYLE (Can't you see how giving and nurturing I am?)

GURU STYLE (Look how wise I am.)

ONE-UPSMAN STYLE (See how cleverly I can put anyone down.)

FAN STYLE (Whatever you do, it's great!)

NICE-GUY STYLE (How could you help but like such a charming, sweet guy as I am?)

DIG-ME STYLE (Don't I entertain and amuse you?)[7]

You may be wondering why some of us take on seemingly productive Acts and others destructive ones. Bradshaw believes that the false self can take many forms.[8] But basically we fall into two groups: the "There is no hope" group, or the "I'll try harder" group.

Those in the "There is no hope" group behave as if they are less than human and take on the form of alcoholics, or slobs, or drug addicts, or doormats, or child-beaters. Clearly, this is the group of us that simply gives up, realizing that there is no way to be perfect.

Those in the "I'll try harder" group behave as if they are more than human, becoming workaholics, or perfectionists, or people-pleasers, or the lives of the party, or do-gooders.

I would suggest a third group, the "I'll do anything to belong" group. Those in this group will adopt any behavior just to fit in. This behavior could be less than human or more than human, depending on the situation. If they are in the company of "tough guys," the "I'll do anything to belong" group takes on an "I am a tough guy" Act. If they are in the company of do-gooders, they take on an "I am doing good" Act. Anything to belong! The irony is that when we twist ourselves in this way, we never have the sense that we truly belong anywhere!

As an exercise, identify as many of your own personal

Acts as you can. You can really have a lot of fun with this if you invite a few caring friends over and spend an evening discussing everyone's favorite Acts. Good friends can help point out some you didn't even know you had! Sharing with others is also a great way to lighten up about what's true for all of us—which is our need to be liked and the lengths to which we will actually go to have that happen. When it's done in the name of love, this process can be very enlightening, indeed!

Note that not all of our Acts are negative. It is our *motivation* that is important. If we are a "nice guy" because of the joy of being a giving person, that's great; but if we are a "nice guy" only because we're desperate to belong, we are unauthentic and immediately prevent true connection from happening. After all, what happens when two actors try to connect? Inevitably, you get a "performance" that looks like connection and sounds like connection, but isn't the real thing.

Once we discover our various Acts for gaining approval, **we must remember not to put ourselves down.** We discover our Acts only to empower ourselves. First we notice: "Ah, yes. There's Susan doing her pleasing-everyone number again. Obviously she isn't feeling good about herself right now." **No self-criticism here—only noticing.** With this observation, we know it's time to pick up our bag of self-esteem tools and put them into practice. Watching ourselves in this way automatically sets the stage for our ultimately letting go of our fake selves.

Again, understand that the processes of discovering and dropping our Acts don't occur overnight. As with all reprogramming activities, the change takes place over a lifetime, as we slowly live more and more into our authenticity. It takes courage to drop our Act. For example, it takes courage to say "no" when our Act is to be a people-pleaser. It take courage to say "please help me" when our Act is to be independent. But with each step we learn to know and like ourselves a little bit more.

ATTEND A CO-DEPENDENTS ANONYMOUS (CODA) MEETING. At last there is a "Twelve-Step program" that benefits us all![9] You may never have had reason to attend any of the Twelve Step programs, such as Alcoholics Anonymous (AA), or Overeaters Anonymous (OA), or Adult Children of Alcoholics (ACA) to name a few. And you may have felt happily left out! But everyone in our society, including you and I, has reason to attend one of the newer Twelve-Step programs—Co-dependents Anonymous (CODA)![9]

Originally, the term "co-dependent" was used to describe someone whose life was enmeshed with an alcoholic, but it's now being described as **a disease of lost self-hood.** In a co-dependent personality, the real self is hidden and the false self is adopted to "fit into" a society that demands unreal behavior on our parts. (Sound familiar?) Some have described it as a dependency on approval from others as one searches for feelings of safety, love, and inner peace.

Co-dependent behavior is often a natural reaction to a dysfunctional family. And I've come to the realization that because of our Somebody Training, by definition . . .

WE ALL COME FROM DYSFUNCTIONAL FAMILIES!

Even if our family appears to be normal and loving, you must understand that our entire society is dysfunctional in its expectations and values. We need only to look around and notice that

Even for those of us who seem to function beautifully in this world, there is a constant struggle to STOP struggling and to live life in spiritual harmony.

Hence we can all benefit from CODA.* CODA is not therapy in the common usage of the term. As with all the Twelve-Step programs, its members take turns in leading meetings. There are no fee or registration requirements. Just show up. The groups meet regularly and at different locations in larger communities. If you don't feel comfortable in one group, try another. Remember that it is common to feel some discomfort initially in any group of strangers. You will feel more at ease as time goes by.

Primarily CODA is a program of learning how to share—to connect. It is designed to help you tell the truth about who you are; to help you take responsibility for your own life without blaming others; to help you love yourself as you deserve to be loved; and to help you trust in a Higher Power (whatever that means for you). Most important, it beautifully demonstrates the reality that "there are no strangers." We are all in it together, all fearful individuals trying very hard in our own way to make it in this seemingly hostile world . . . all trying to learn how to make the world more peaceful and loving for ourselves and others.

TRY SOME "INNER-CHILD" WORK. Since so many of our problems of self-esteem and dependency start

---

*NOTE: It you are in therapy, consult your therapist before attending a CODA meeting, or any group meeting for that matter.

when we are young and are carried with us—consciously or unconsciously—all through life, we need to find a way of going back and correcting the implanted "errors" in our thinking so that we can let go of our destructive patterns of behavior. Inner-child workshops are springing up all over the country as a way of getting us back to where the trouble began and reprogramming ourselves into a more loving way of seeing ourselves. See if any such workshops are available in your area and if they seem right for you. Also, more and more books are being written that deal with healing the inner child.[10]

PLANT SEEDS OF SELF-RESPECT. All of us, at times, behave in ways that take away our self-respect. One obvious way is drinking too much. Other ways are less obvious. For example, when we are dependent personalities (and, remember, we all are!), we create "connection-killers" that lower our self-respect. These include anger, judgment, manipulation, impossible expectations, helplessness, envy, jealousy, self-righteousness, super-independence, and lack of commitment.

It is important that, **without blaming ourselves,** we become **observers** of what we do to lower our self-respect. And then it is important that we act in a manner that raises it. Here's the magic formula:

> **When you put loving thoughts and behavior into the world, you plant seeds of self-respect. When you put unloving thoughts and behavior into the world, you destroy seeds of self-respect.**

Simple, isn't it? At least in principle. Not so simple in execution. Loving ourselves and others is **impossible** to do all the time. Our internal Chatterbox is always there

to introduce fearful thoughts that take away our ability
love. But as we continue on the path toward our High
Self, the balance improves—the number of loving acts in-
creases and the number of unloving acts decreases. Putting
out loving thoughts and behavior does not mean that we
allow others to walk all over us. In fact, when we let others
walk over us, we are killing our self-respect.

Nothing is as unattractive as footprints on the face!

When we stand tall and respect who we are, we naturally
open our hearts and draw more beautiful people into our
lives. Always remember that **like attracts like.** With
open hearts, we draw open hearts into our lives. With
closed hearts, we draw closed hearts.

One way to plant seeds of self-respect is to volunteer to
work for a charity or cause in which you believe. Nothing
does more to create a feeling of self-respect than being a
helping force. The satisfaction can be enormous. Volunteering reduces the self-absorption that creates a sense of
isolation and directs our attention to others, thereby helping us feel more at home in the world.

I suggest you take out a pen and pad and answer the
question "What makes me feel great about myself and what
doesn't?" Look at your life and write down how you can
systematically begin to root out the seeds of self-destruction
and replace them with seeds of self-respect. Give these
seeds the time to take root and grow, and soon you will see
a beautiful garden that represents the best of who you are.

Again, don't be impatient. **Note every step forward,**
no matter how big or small. At some point during each day,
take a few minutes to write down all the ways you have
added to the light that warms the world. Write down every

compliment and thank-you you utter, every nice thought you think, every time you lend a helping hand, every time you validate others and make them feel good about themselves.

With each acknowledgment of your own inner beauty, you soothe the hurt within. Only you can create the experience of self-worth for yourself. No one out there can create it for you. And once you've got it, no one can take it away.

4

Healing the Lonely Heart

Loneliness is a feeling that can lead us toward greater exploration of who we truly are and what we have to give to this world, and thus toward authentic connection. Or it can lead to self-destructive actions in our desperate attempts to fill the emptiness inside.

Whether loneliness is enriching or destructive in our lives depends on our willingness to pick up the mirror and look it squarely in the eye. Sometimes this is difficult, because loneliness is too often an emotion we mask from ourselves. There are an amazing number of escape routes which we take to avoid or deny feeling lonely: workaholism, drug addiction, a whirlwind of social activities, hasty marriages, dehumanizing sexual encounters, blasting radios or televisions, living in the past, or restlessness. This is understandable: loneliness can be very painful. But when it is hidden, it becomes our master, and we are but robots trading our

51

aliveness for imagined safety. When it is out in the open, we become its master and use it as a stepping stone toward greater fulfillment.

Where does all this loneliness come from? Most experts would agree that loneliness is felt in infancy, as we begin to experience our own separateness. Experts do not agree, however, as to why it persists. Their observations revolve around three categories: 1) **physical separation;** 2) **emotional separation;** and 3) **spiritual separation.**

1. PHYSICAL SEPARATION. There is very little sense of permanence or continuity in today's world. By definition, a technological society creates separation and isolation. It allows an enormous amount of physical mobility, and as a result, family members are often scattered all over the country, even the world. The divorce rate is higher than it has ever been, leaving family members torn apart from the security of the family unit. Society also allows tremendous job mobility, so that we are constantly facing new challenges and new co-workers. Some even work at home—alone—with the "company" of their fax machine and computer.

As a result, life requires many good-byes to that which is familiar as we make our move from place to place, job to job, situation to situation, house to house, and person to person. Hence, some of our loneliness logically comes from our feeling of having no roots, no community. **In fact, it is a tribute to our adaptability that we human beings cope as well as we do!**

A second type of physical separation results from the fact that so many people are shy about inviting others into their lives. As a result, they find themselves without companionship. Many people complain that they never meet people or get invited anywhere, and there they sit, wondering why they are so alone. They are alone because they're not making an effort to reach out to other people: instead they are hoping and praying that someone will reach out to them. And that's not the way the world usually works.

When we depend on the world to invite us in, we create a situation in which we are always on the outside looking in, yearning to be a part of the warmth that lies in someone else's heart.

A third type of physical separation is created by our alienation from nature. City living, in particular, makes us lose touch with the connectedness of all life. Thus we are oblivious to the destructive consequences of our actions upon the very thing that gives us life. Our abuse of our planet reflects our loss of self. People are now becoming much more concerned about the environment. Along with this concern comes an observable shift from Somebody Trained separateness to Everybody Trained togetherness. In the pulling together for a common good, we begin to taste the deliciousness of what oneness on the planet could feel like. As we come to feel a sense of global community, some of our feelings of alienation will be replaced by a feeling of belonging.

2. EMOTIONAL SEPARATION. Counselor Ira Tanner suggests it is not physical but emotional separation from people that creates loneliness.[1] It was a great revelation to him in his marriage and family practice to find that **the most intense loneliness is found within a home in which there is no communication.** While we may have the physical closeness of a family, silent dinners and walled-off hearts between family members can create an agonizing sense of loneliness.

Loneliness is often the result of a closed heart. Our fear of being hurt, rejected, or judged keeps us frozen in our loneliness. We are not able to open our hearts enough to allow in the warmth of others, which would melt the pain we feel inside. We blame someone "out there" for our isolation, not realizing that our internal walls are responsible for our pain, not the actions of others.

In that place of pain and blame, we become psychologically numb to the feelings of others. We can't feel *their* pain. We can't feel *their* fear. We can't feel *their* loneliness. That is, we can feel no empathy—which is a great glue for connection! When we feel empathy, the walls come tumbling down, and what was once "me versus you" becomes "us together." When we let go of the fear and pain, and open ourselves to others, much of the loneliness disappears.

Another reason for our loneliness is the loss of our authentic self as we struggle to conform to society's standards. No wonder we are lonely; when we look inside, it feels like there's nobody home. No wonder we glom on to someone "out there" to move in with, literally and figuratively. This is only our desperate attempt to find a place where there really *is* someone home.

3. SPIRITUAL SEPARATION.   Spiritual separation has to do with our loss of connection with our Higher Self. Whether we believe in God or not, it is critical that we develop a strong inner spiritual connection, a deep, abiding sense of our own inner power and integrity. When we are not on that path toward inner connection, we experience a heart aching to be healed. And it is healed not by the actions that our Somebody Training asks us to take but rather by the actions that our Everybody Training asks us to take.

Our heart is healed only through loving, caring, opening, sharing, helping, giving, feeling, embracing, and warming the world with our love.

As you can see, the reasons for our loneliness are varied and so are the many things we can do to begin filling the emptiness we feel inside. Let me remind you once again that this is a step-by-step process. It doesn't happen in one giant leap. Have patience and let a sense of inner peace and fulfillment unfold—all in its own time.

"FILLING-THE-EMPTINESS" EXERCISES

LEARN THE FULLNESS OF SOLITUDE. In order to truly handle our loneliness, it is critical that we learn how to be comfortable with solitude. Many of us are not, even if we live alone. The minute we walk in the door, we look to the blare of the radio or television to give us the sense that we are not really alone. Or we pick up the telephone to connect us with a feeling of safety. We avoid being alone for the obvious reason that it can be very painful. And it is this avoidance that keeps us from learning how to feel full in the midst of solitude. What can you do to change the pattern? The following exercise is a good start.

A. Take some time to sit in silence. Whenever you have the addictive need to turn on the radio or television or call a friend, simply stop yourself, and let the feelings under the emptiness come up. The real enemy is not the loneliness, **but the avoidance of loneliness.**

B. Allow part of your mind to become the observer of what is going on. That means, watch yourself sitting there experiencing whatever emotions come up. "Oh, there's Susan feeling lonely again." What happens when you do this is that you get to see that **it is only one part of you that is lonely, not all of you.** Let me illustrate: When you began the exercise there was only . . .

LONELY ME

at which point, you felt trapped in the middle of the loneliness. Then, when you became the observer, the situation became

LONELY ME   ME WATCHING
                       LONELY ME

Already you are less lonely, as now there are two of you! What you've done is put a little wedge into that sense of being trapped in your isolation. Taking this step distances us from painful feelings so we are not consumed by them. We learn that we are *more* than "lonely me" (or any other emotion we are feeling). Now, as you sit there watching the feelings come up you can take it a step further.

C. Jot your thoughts down on a piece of paper. Writing really helps ease pain and clarify thoughts. Save your notes, being sure to date each one. Given enough time, you will be able to arrange them in chronological order and have the satisfaction of reviewing the immense amount of growth you have attained.

D. Start with a set amount of time in which you are going to sit in silence, and gradually increase it. At the beginning, you may want to sit on your own for only five minutes. The amount of time doesn't matter. As in all human-growth activities it is important to **begin where you are.** Trying to do too much at one time is a self-defeating mechanism that guarantees failure. Each day, slowly increase your time alone, until you feel comfortable just sitting there writing down your thoughts for at least one-half hour, or more if you so choose.

E. To comfort yourself, remember why the feeling of loneliness has come up. The reason the loneliness is there is simply because you are giving up your traditional escapes and support systems. You are moving your life support from *outer* to *inner* and, for a while, it will feel as though support is nowhere to be found. It may feel a bit like withdrawal symptoms, whether from a drug, a schedule, or an attitude. You're on your own without anesthesia, and that can be very scary and painful at first. Just go with it.

F. When your allotted time is up, notice that you handled any feelings that came up. As soon as you see that you won't die from your loneliness (and you won't), you'll say, "Hey, I handled that! I can handle it again."

G. Plan the next time for sitting with your solitude. It is something that needs to be repeated incrementally and systematically. It is a reconditioning process and as such it takes time to transform the experience from pain to power. Believe it or not, as you make this "loneliness" activity part of your routine . . .

The day will come when you will sit there and notice that loneliness doesn't come up any more.

You will have faced that inner demon and realized that you were stronger than it was. That in itself is incredibly empowering. If you follow this process, you will be well on your way to discovering the joy of solitude.

CREATE SOME NOURISHING ALONE-TIME ACTIVITIES IN YOUR HOME.   Most of us don't allow ourselves any time to leisurely read a book, meditate, take a long hot bath, listen to inspirational tapes, cook a wonderful meal just for ourselves (if we like to cook), light the candles, and enjoy peace and solitude. It is imperative that we begin to . . .

Slow down and listen to the voice within that connects us all.

To make these times alone even more pleasurable, **prepare for them, look forward to them, and make them a choice instead of a penance!**

If you have children, and rarely find yourself with the luxury of an empty house or free time, trade baby-sitting time with a friend so you can have some solitude at regular intervals. If you are married, encourage your mate to spend an occasional evening out with a friend. If you have a roommate, take advantage of those times when he (or she) is off doing something on his own. There is always a way to create a little piece of solitude in our busy lives.

Make this date with yourself a priority. An invitation from a friend coinciding with time you'd planned to spend alone may seem very tempting, especially in the beginning when spending time alone may still feel uncomfortable; but remember that learning how to be alone is an important step in learning to connect. Explain to your friend, "I have a very important date—with myself."

There was a point in my life, between marriages, when I made it a practice not to accept any invitations from Friday night to Sunday night. And for me, Saturday night was *not* the loneliest night in the week, as the old song of my youth suggests. It became the richest!

Constant activity in the outside world, without the balance of inner activity, contributes to our loneliness. We end up separating ourselves from the very thing that gives us peace.

Feeling comfortable on your own takes some time. Allow yourself the discomfort that comes up for you. You will notice that slowly, but surely, the dread will be replaced by a feeling of happy anticipation.

MAKE YOUR HOME A HEALING RETREAT.
Take a very long look at the place that you call home. Does it represent the best in you? Does it give you a feeling of peace? Does it symbolize your love for yourself?

For so many people, the home they live in is a reflection of the emptiness they feel inside. For example, I have been in the homes of men and women who are divorced, and it was hard to believe the sense of separation rather than connection that pervaded the space. One man had been divorced for four years, yet boxes from his move out of his marital home still cluttered the living room and bedroom. Who would ever want to come home to such reminders of endings, instead of new beginnings?

Others live in homes that are far beneath the standard of what they want to enjoy. They claim to be waiting for someone to come along—and then they'll fix up the place or move somewhere better. What a waste! They could be surrounding themselves with symbols of self-love right now! Why wait? Create a home that you look forward to coming home to. It doesn't require a lot of money to do that. It requires creativity and self-respect.

If you have roommates who don't share your desire to improve your home, choose one room, perhaps your bedroom, to make your sanctuary. Or find a new roommate. If you have children who constantly invade your privacy, there is always a little corner of the house that you can call your own. We all need a little refuge from those people or things that demand a part of us. We need to create a place of peace where we can put ourselves back together again when we start feeling fragmented in a world full of stress.

DO THINGS OUTSIDE THE HOUSE BY YOURSELF.
The world can be a friendly place, or it can be hostile. The critical factor is our attitude. If we think the world will treat us badly, we close our doors, thus plunging ourselves into darkness. If we think the world will embrace us lovingly, we open our doors and step into a world filled with enlightening experiences.

Here are a few activities that I found very valuable in my journey to wholeness.

A. Acclimate yourself to eating alone in restaurants. In the beginning, this can feel very uncomfortable, particularly for women. This is because we have been told that women are not treated well if they eat alone in a restaurant. Of course, any such restaurant will simply lose you as a customer! However, I have never been treated badly eating alone in a restaurant! And I eat out alone all over the world!

During all the years I was single, I often ate out alone; and now when my husband has an evening meeting or when I am on a lecture tour, I eat out alone. And I love it. What do I do? I people-watch, I think, I write, I read, and I truly dine. I don't rush. Sometimes I linger longer on my own than I would with friends or family. It doesn't have to be an expensive restaurant. Good food, a quiet place, and friendly service are what you want. Again, in the beginning, eating out alone can be an uncomfortable experience, but it will become one that you find very nourishing, in more ways than one.

B. Take short trips into nature on your own. One of my favorite activities when I was single was to take long weekend trips to the beach. I would rent a little beach cabin that belonged to one of the hotels, bring a stack of books, and talk to no one, just enjoying the peace for the entire time.

To enhance the feeling of solitude, I always went there in the dead of winter when everything was deserted. I would walk alone on the beach, all bundled up, and at times I felt myself profoundly connected to the entire Universe. There were moments that I actually felt the presence of God all around me. Some of the most powerful experiences in my life happened during these times alone. They provided me with some stunningly beautiful insights about life and growth. **Yes, at times it was scary and lonely.** But the rewards were monumental.

A lovely book that describes this kind of experience is *A Gift From the Sea* by Anne Morrow Lindbergh, written at a time when women did not have the choices they have today. In that sense, it is a bit dated, but its message still applies. Lindbergh would leave her five children and husband to go off to a deserted island by herself for a few weeks each year. She says that the parting was the most painful of all—like an amputation. Yet the rewards made up for it.

> "Life rushes back into the void, richer, more vivid, fuller than before. It is as if in parting one did actually lose an arm. And then, like the star-fish, one grows it anew; one is whole again, complete and round—more whole, even, than before, when the other people had pieces of one."[2]

Yes, nature can present us with our most sublime moments. As I look back on my life, I realize that the key turning points in my quest for wholeness all occurred when I created moments for myself in quiet places in nature—on the beach, on a mountaintop, or looking up at the stars. In the past I have always chosen big-city living, but my husband and I recently made the move to a place of wondrous natural beauty that provides more solitude.

C. Travel "alone" with a tour group of people with similar interests. I can hear the groans as images of tour buses and tourists with cameras around their necks cross before your eyes. Yes, that's what the tour groups look like! But there is more than meets the eye.

When I was single, I wanted to travel, but I didn't want to be all alone in exotic new lands where I didn't speak the language. So I'd find special-interest tours that were very reasonable in price and very wonderful in their possibilities for self-growth. For example, I traveled with a group of meditators to Egypt and a group of health professionals to Cuba.

I purposely did not invite friends on these trips because I knew I would not reach out to others the way I would if I were on my own. Also, a companion wouldn't have allowed the time alone I relished. At many points in our tour-directed day, I would drop out and go exploring on my own and, as a result, had some incredibly wonderful experiences. Yet the group was always available, a great consolation in a place where the language and customs were alien to me.

The reason I emphasize special-interest tours is that common interests offer an immediate point of connection. Also, these tours usually take one off the well-beaten path of regular tours into areas that might be more of interest to you. For example, when I went to India with a Jain monk and some of his disciples, I was able to see magical parts of the Indian culture that I would have never experienced on a regular tour. Special-interest group tours, involving art, music, geology, or almost any interest, abound. Start at the travel bureau, ask colleagues, and buy travel magazines. Before embarking on such an adventure, check out the people who are organizing the tour. Even better, ask to talk to someone who has already made a trip with them.

And remember this: Because we all have fear of the unknown (and travel is definitely an unknown), your body and mind may create much resistance to such a trip. For example, I often found myself with the flu a week before a scheduled trip. I would simply tell my body, "Even if you have to be driven to the airport in an ambulance, you are going on this trip." I always made it to the airport!

Once I got there, I would look at the congregating group and decide that they were all boring and horrible and that

I would absolutely hate the trip! Of course, I ended up loving most of them and feeling very sad on the last night at the prospect of saying our good-byes. Tours have an intensity that creates a very strong bonding with people. I carry with me today many wonderful memories of these extraordinary trips into the unknown.

LEARN THE HEALING POWER OF MEDITA-TION. Meditation is a wonderful way of connecting with the self. There are various forms of meditation, for example Zen, Tibetan, and Transcendental. They are all well worth your investigation. There are an enormous number of books on the subject and most likely there are classes to attend in your area. The purpose of meditation is to quiet the chatter in the mind and transcend to a realm of peace. I am so impressed with the power of meditation that I have created a special meditation area in my home.

As a way of calming us, meditation teaches us about breathing. Most of us are shallow breathers, yet it is through deeper breathing that we become relaxed and open to taking in the beauty around us. Proper breathing allows the fullness of inner and outer flow, enabling us to see our connectedness with all that is. Take a deep breath right now, and notice how it relaxes you.

Meditation also allows us to see the bigger picture. When the mind is cluttered, we only see ourselves as fragmented and tired human beings. When the mind is at peace, we see ourselves floating in a sea of harmony. In life, we must strive for a balance between solitude and involvement. In fact, the secret of handling the stress that is a natural part of most of our lives lies in the moments when we return to the peace of the Higher Self. It is here that we often find answers to pressing problems. As theologian Henri J. M. Nouwen so beautifully says . . .

> It is in solitude that we discover that being is more important than having, and that we are worth more than the result of our efforts. In solitude, we discover that our life is not a possession to be defended, but a gift to be shared.[3]

As you learn your life is a gift to be shared, you can feel more comfortable inviting others into your life.

MAKE THE FIRST MOVE.   Many of us lament the fact that we are often alone. We live with the illusion that there is no one out there to fill the empty spaces. The truth is

**There really is NEVER a need to be alone
if you don't want to be.**

There are many people out there who would joyfully share our lives. We just have to invite them in. Don't expect them to invite you into their world. They may or they may not. If they do, that's pure gravy. But it's really up to you.

Invite someone to have lunch or dinner or go to a movie with you. **Don't expect him or her to invite you.**

Knock on your neighbors' door and invite them in for a cup of coffee. If they're not home, leave them a note to call you. **Don't expect him or her to invite you.**

Think about what you love to do and take some classes that revolve around these activities. Invite someone in the class to an activity that is related to this particular shared interest. **Don't expect him or her to invite you.**

After a weekend workshop, YOU make the suggestion that everyone get together at your house for a reunion. **Don't expect them to invite you.**

See yourself at the center of your own Universe, into which you want to invite others. Always take the responsibility for taking the first move . . . and the second and third and fourth, if necessary. I always keep in mind two quotes which I heard many years ago. Put them both wherever they will serve as a constant reminder:

BE THE HOST IN LIFE, NOT THE GUEST.

and

DON'T WARM YOURSELF BY THE FIRE;
BE THE ONE TO LIGHT IT!

This doesn't mean that you won't ever be invited to share activities with others; of course you will. Nor does it mean that you can't sometimes just sit there and be the recipient of someone else's warmth; of course you can. The point is **always to be responsible for your own good time.**

In line with being the host in life, and not the guest, you can see how there is never an excuse for being alone on your birthday or Christmas or New Year's Eve or whatever . . . not when you are creating the party!

Once again, notice the control this puts in your hands, not in someone else's. Extend the hand of friendship to many people so that if a few disappoint you, there are always others. There is a wonderful old adage: "Have at least eight friends. If you need something, seven of them will be busy!"

Remember, there is no shortage of potential friends.

There are probably only a few million people in your immediate area that would greatly welcome your companionship! If you live in a small town, the numbers may be smaller, but the principle is the same. The chapters to come contain some helpful tools to push through the fear of making those first moves.

JOIN A SPECIAL-INTEREST GROUP. When my husband and I moved to Los Angeles, we knew very few people there. Since so much of what I do professionally and personally revolves around the spiritual journey, I was interested in finding a like-minded group of people with whom to learn and grow. One day, I heard of The Inside Edge, a group that meets for breakfast once a week, during which guest speakers share their ideas about bringing the values of love and caring into all of life's activities. Aside from the breakfast meetings, there are many other Edge activities, such as a men's group, a business group, a writer's group, a woman's group, and a dance group, and many social events as well.[4] It sounded perfect . . . and it was. My husband and I joined and in a very short time we felt connected to the other 150 like-minded people that comprised the group.

Understand that the feeling of connection we felt did not happen in an instant. In fact, the first few times my husband and I attended the breakfast meetings, we felt very much like outsiders looking in. But **as we actively participated and volunteered** in the many activities which stemmed from the core breakfast meetings, we began to get a wonderful sense of belonging. A warmer group of people would be hard to find, yet **it was our INVOLVEMENT in the group that created our positive feelings.**

After I had been a member of the group for about a year,

I encouraged an acquaintance of mine to join, as she constantly complained that it was hard to meet people and Los Angeles was such a lonely place. Week after week and event after event she appeared, but never really participated. She complained that no one ever included her in anything. I explained that it isn't about "being included in" anything, it's about extending yourself outward. Still, she kept waiting for the group to "give" her something. She never understood the "law of getting" is a direct result of the "law of giving." And she truly gave nothing of herself. I suspect the reason, sadly, is that she never realized how much she had to give. True to form, she soon began finding fault with everyone and everything around her . . . just as she did in life outside the group. Eventually, of course, she dropped out, thereby missing an opportunity to spend time with many fine people.

There are many types of groups you can join—for example, political, religious, sport, spiritual, art, charitable, nature, or environmental. When you join a special-interest group of any kind, become part of the group by **volunteering, inviting, creating, caring, sharing, giving, and loving.** You can then carry this principle of involvement out to the world at large, knowing that . . .

It is your involvement with the world that makes you feel you truly belong.

Given all that we can do to fill the empty space created by our loneliness, I believe that even those who have learned to be comfortable within themselves and comfortable reaching out to others still experience a degree of loneliness in the depth of their being . . . something beyond the everyday loneliness of wanting to have someone to go to the movies with. I once wrote a poem:

**My life is beautiful,
I have it all . . .
But even in the sunshine,
One has to cry sometimes.**

As I look back to the time I wrote those words, I realize I was talking about the tears of loneliness—the kind of cosmic loneliness that comes from the realization of the awesome vastness of the universe and our inability to understand it all. Once we have connected with ourselves, we can be at peace with this kind of loneliness, and recognize it as a beautiful part of the human experience that actually enhances our life.

Loneliness can be beautiful when it keeps us moving upward to greater heights of awareness . . . when it pulls us forward to learn, to seek, to grow. As long as we use it as a tool for self-discovery, loneliness has magical results. Knowing it is a call forward, we should not be upset at its presence in our lives. We should just heed its call and ask ourselves how we can move forward into wholeness and love. There is nothing wrong with us when we feel our loneliness. We are not misfits or losers. We are incurably and wonderfully human.

THE JOURNEY OUTWARD
TO CONNECTION

5

That First Hello!
"The Essentials of Connection"

Imagine yourself standing at the door of an unfamiliar room, facing a room full of "strangers" and feeling very nervous indeed. The occasion could be purely social or in some way related to business. As you stand there feeling like the outsider looking in, the voice of the internal (and eternal!) Chatterbox is most likely telling you some version of the following:

> I don't see a soul that I know. They all look like they know each other. I hope someone will talk to me. I'm overdressed. I look fat. Maybe I'd better go and check my hair. I feel so nervous. I hope I don't have to shake hands with anyone . . . my palms are all sweaty. I feel so lost. Everyone else seems to be so comfortable. I wish I could leave.

Even if your Chatterbox is on good behavior and remaining mercifully quiet, you still can't ignore the quickened heartbeat, the churning stomach, or however your nervousness makes itself felt.

How can we overcome these feelings of discomfort? Can we ever learn to look into a room full of people and simply decide to have a wonderful time connecting with everyone we meet? Or for that matter, is it possible to approach *all* situations—whether involving one person or one thousand—knowing that there is nothing to fear? The answer is a definite *yes*! Many basic tools and concepts are available to make us feel more comfortable in that metaphoric crowded room (or job interview, blind date, or introduction to your future mother-in-law).

But first, let's review some of the important differences between Somebody Training and Everybody Training.

SOMEBODY TRAINING TEACHES US TO . . .	EVERYBODY TRAINING TEACHES US TO . . .
WORK ON WHAT'S OUTSIDE	WORK ON WHAT'S INSIDE
SEE HOW MUCH WE CAN GET	SEE HOW MUCH WE CAN GIVE
DEVELOP A WINNING ACT	DISCOVER THE AUTHENTIC SELF
IGNORE THE HIGHER SELF	ACT FROM THE HIGHER SELF
CONTROL THE ACTIONS AND REACTIONS OF OTHERS	CONTROL OUR OWN ACTIONS AND REACTIONS

It is obvious that any tools and concepts of connection that derive from Somebody Training have a different focus than those that come from Everybody Training. Most techniques featured in magazines, and many self-help books, are of the Somebody Training variety. They offer help . . . but only on a very superficial level. The reason for this is that, by definition . . .

Any tool coming from our Somebody Training is inherently a tool of separation rather than one of connection.

Somebody Training techniques will always in some way teach us about competition and game playing, about getting something from someone else, and about masking who we truly are. Hence, they serve ultimately to increase fear rather than diminish it. Somebody Training techniques would include:

dressing to kill; playing it cool; not appearing too anxious; impressing everyone with your money, success, or chest size; acting coy; acting "manly"; acting with bravado; acting; acting; and acting!

God forbid that anyone should see us as we truly are!

A recent magazine article telling us how to make a great impression offered such tips as using a breath mint; keeping an expensive pen in your pocket or purse; wearing expensive shoes; and not wearing too much makeup. Hardly tips that build one's confidence! In our society, tips like these may indeed help to create just the kind of initial impression you are looking for. There are a few problems with suggestions such as these, however.

Problem #1 is that the message to our conscious and subconscious mind is always "You're not good enough the way you truly are and if you don't do something to cover up all those flaws, you won't be acceptable to anyone!" Subtly or not so subtly, we're being told that our genuine selves are not attractive, and that we need external "props" to make the grade. You may argue, "I don't care about the subconscious message! I need help and if these techniques work, I'll try them!" This leads us to problem #2.

Problem #2 is that Somebody Training techniques work only temporarily. They never address the root cause of your fears. What happens beyond that first hello? You're still the "you" who doesn't feel good enough. You still stand nervously on guard for fear that the "real" you may come seeping out! Hardly a good basis for authentic connection! In fact, many people begin a relationship, date, marry, and live the rest of their lives standing guard at the door of their authentic self for fear that who they really are is simply not good enough. And if their mate ever found out who they really are, he or she would probably leave. So many people are afraid of "being found out"—and this is why!

Let's move on to some techniques of the Everybody Training variety and see how they differ. Remember the original scenario. There you are standing in an unfamiliar room full of "strangers," and, despite the breath mint and the expensive shoes, feeling very nervous indeed. The negative internal Chatterbox is blabbering away, evaporating every ounce of confidence that you may have mustered. It's now time for step #1.

STEP 1: SAY "STOP!" TO THE CHATTERBOX!
That powerful little word is a shortened version of the following:

STOP! I'M SICK AND TIRED OF THIS AND I WON'T TAKE IT ANYMORE! I'M REPLACING YOU WITH A VOICE THAT RESPECTS WHO I AM!

You will automatically experience a moment of blessed silence within your head. That's the moment to quickly implement the next step #2.

STEP 2: REPLACE THE NEGATIVITY OF THE CHATTERBOX WITH THE SELF-CARING TALK THAT COMES FROM THE HIGHER SELF. Here is a perfect place and time to use our affirmations, which serve to remind us of our worth. So, after telling our Chatterbox to stop, we begin repeating to ourselves at least ten times in quick succession such positive statements as . . .

I am a pleasure to know.

I am proud of who I am.

I am a lovable person.

I have much to give.

I bring light wherever I go.

Again, the mere saying of these words will begin to make you feel better about yourself and your situation. Remember, you don't have to believe affirmations in order for them to work. Your subconscious mind will absorb them and that is the most important thing. As you repeat the affirmations, you will notice that you are standing a little taller and feeling a bit calmer. Trust me on this one!

You're then ready to move into the room and focus on

a person or a group of people with whom you would like to connect. It is now time for step #3.

STEP 3: ASSURE YOURSELF THAT NO MATTER WHAT RESPONSE YOU GET FROM ANYONE YOU MEET, YOU ARE A WORTHWHILE PERSON!

Read this once again. It is a very important clue as to why we are so afraid to approach another person. We assume that our worth is tied up in the way other people—even so-called "strangers"—treat us. This simply is not true. Your worth depends on what *YOU* think of you! And, of course, that's part of the problem! Repeat the following statement:

> **No matter how *anyone* reacts to me,**
> **I know I am a worthwhile person.**

The implication of this statement is profound! Think about it. It means that you're not going to let anyone else determine your worth; it means that the only person in charge of how you feel about yourself is YOU; it means that you are breaking your need-for-approval-from-others habit which has run you for too long; it means that you are silencing the Chatterbox and letting your Higher Self determine your personal worth. A pretty powerful statement, I would say!

STEP 4: WALK UP AND GREET THE PERSON YOU ARE INTERESTED IN GETTING TO KNOW.

I use the word *greet* purposely as it describes exactly what you want to do. My trusty thesaurus tells me that to "greet" means to "acknowledge, salute, welcome, hail, and receive." Translated into the kind of words that come from the Higher Self, this means . . .

I acknowledge your presence.

I salute your humanness.

I welcome what you have to offer this world.

I hail the beauty in you.

I receive you with a loving heart.

In case this all sounds very bizarre, remember, this is Higher Self language, a far different cry from the Chatterbox which would be saying . . .

I want him (or her) to acknowledge my presence.

I want him to salute my humanness.

I want her to acknowledge what I have to offer this world.

I want him to hail the beauty within me.

I want her to receive me with a loving heart.

This kind of thinking brings terror into our hearts. What if no one does any of the above? Remember, there is never a guarantee that you will get the results you are seeking. The only guaranteed way of getting results that empower instead of destroy is to imprint in your mind your Higher Self message that "no matter how anyone speaks to me, I am a worthwhile person. My sense of self depends on no one else."

Remember that we never have control over other people. We do have control over what we think and do in this world. And it is far more nourishing to "think and do" in the language of self-love and self-respect, which comes from Everybody Training techniques. To strengthen your resolve when you approach another person in a caring manner and are fearful they will treat you badly, remember . . .

Whatever the situation, the more hurtfully or obnoxiously a person acts toward you, the smaller he (or she) feels inside, the more out of touch he is with his own inherent beauty, and the more psychologically numb he is to the feelings of other people. His ACT of superiority is inevitably his attempt to hide his own humiliating lack of self-worth.

Hang the above paragraph on your wall if you have to. It is true! Everyone has their out-of-sorts moments, of course, but generally speaking, anyone who is in touch with their own self-worth acts in a kind manner to everyone around him or her.

Now that you are standing before him (or her), what then?

STEP 5: LOOK HIM IN THE EYE WHILE SILENTLY PROJECTING CARING THOUGHTS.

In one of my workshops, I use an Everybody Training connection exercise which students report has helped them break down their discomfort in all manner of social and business encounters. While it is in itself an artificial situation, I will show you later how to apply the general principles in your everyday activities.

First, I ask everyone in the room, all "strangers" to each other up until now, to find a partner and stand facing each other. (It's at this point that I usually lose one person to the rest room . . . his or her fear is just too great!) When the rest of the class members, however reluctantly, have all found partners, I give them the following instructions: "Look into your partner's eyes. No smiling and no talking allowed. And as you do this, I want you to silently project the following thought:"

THIS IS A PERSON JUST LIKE ME . . . A HUMAN BEING WITH FEELINGS . . . WHO WANTS TO CONNECT . . . WHO WANTS TO BE LIKED . . . WHO HAS ALSO FACED THE PAIN OF REJECTION AT TIMES . . . AND WHO IS JUST AS NERVOUS AS I AM.

As they are projecting this Everybody Training thought, I remind them again to look into each other's eyes and just BE. Nothing to do, nothing to say . . . just BE! Sounds easy, right? Wrong! It is amazing how difficult it is for some people to do this part of the exercise. Many find the need to smile, or joke, or talk. To look into another person's eyes and just BE is very threatening.

If their Chatterbox is rearing its nasty little head and offering such unhelpful statements as "I wish I had put on more eye makeup today," I tell them to notice these thoughts, let them go, and concentrate on projecting the Everybody Training thoughts I gave them. I remind them that connection truly begins telepathically. The thoughts we project set the stage for much of what will happen later.

After a few moments, I say: "Now I'd like you to smile while still maintaining eye contact. And with your smile, silently project the following thought to your partner":

I'D REALLY LIKE TO GET TO KNOW YOU. I WOULD LIKE TO SHARE THE BEST OF WHO I AM WITH THE BEST OF WHO YOU ARE. I WOULD LIKE TO SUPPORT YOU IN FEELING GREAT ABOUT YOURSELF. I WOULD LIKE TO

BE YOUR FRIEND. I APPRECIATE THE ESSENCE OF WHO YOU ARE.

After a few more moments they are instructed as follows: "Now I'd like you to hug each other, really sharing your warmth with your partner and taking in the warmth they have to offer you. Feel yourself melting into the hug, truly relaxing into each other's warmth, and silently project the following thought":

I GIVE YOU WARMTH AND COMFORT AS I TAKE IN THE WARMTH AND COMFORT YOU GIVE TO ME.

And finally, after a few moments, I give them the signal to break apart and thank each other for being their partner.

There is a definite sense of relief in the room as they begin to feel "Boy, I'm glad this is over." But the relief turns to discomfort again as I quickly tell them to pick another partner. I hear a few groans, but they comply. I repeat this process again a minimum of six times, sometimes with partners of the same sex and sometimes with partners of the opposite sex. And, lo and behold, with each change of partners, **the tension in the room diminishes noticeably.**

When the process is over and they return to their seats, it is interesting to notice the changed energy of everyone in the class (except, of course, for the fearful person who is just returning from the rest room). Their initial discomfort has been transformed into joyful familiarity. Everyone is laughing and chatting with his or her neighbor. **A sense of connection has permeated the room.**

I point out to them the contrast between this scene and the earlier one when they began filtering into the room before class began. One by one they entered the room, looked around sheepishly, and then chose a seat as far away from everyone else as possible. As more and more people came into the room, they had no choice but to sit next to one another. And that is all they did . . . they sat! Discomfort and tension were clearly in the air. Except for a few whispers between those who had brought along a friend, not a word was spoken.

And now, after the connection exercise, I have trouble restoring quiet, they are so busy comparing notes with one another. When they are finally calmed down, I go around the room asking everyone to share the thoughts they had as they were going through the exercise. Here are a few of the responses:

In the beginning I wanted to disappear. And then it got easier.

It was hard to just be. I had to giggle, make a joke.

I find with glasses I feel detached. Maybe they are a barrier.

You certainly feel closer to everyone.

The smile eased the situation. It felt more comfortable.

I thought "Oh, God, I wish I didn't have this zit." I really felt self-conscious.

It got easier with practice. I was really nervous to begin with, but by the end of the process, I even looked forward to my next partner.

I was so caught up in my own discomfort I noticed that it was hard to get into the other person.

After about thirty seconds, amazing things started to happen. I fell in love at least three times!

I enjoyed watching people become more comfortable as I became more comfortable than them. It gave me a powerful feeling.

It is always fascinating to me to watch the varied reactions as my students move through the process. As I said earlier, without practice it is very difficult for people to look each other in the eyes without smiling or talking. The discomfort of just *being* is enormous. Most of the class feels a need to *do* something . . . such as smile, giggle, make a joke, make a sexy remark, or tell their partner he (or she) has pretty eyes. Even the most outgoing among us have some difficulty with eyeball-to-eyeball contact.

And then there are the hugs. Some really get in there with their softness and warmth. Others are so rigid that no warmth is allowed out—and, sadly, none is allowed in. Men find it extremely difficult to hug other men, so you hear a lot of backslapping and jokes. It's really hard for them to show genuine affection without being a bit "manly" about it. (I'll speak to this issue in Chapter 8.)

As I stated earlier, this connection exercise is artificial, yet its principles can work with anyone at anytime in any place. Since you have not had the benefit of practicing the Everybody Training connection exercise in one of my classes, I've come up with the following plan which will give similar results:

First, as you walk down the street, or shop, or engage in any activity where there are people around you, start really "seeing" other people as you probably have never seen them before. We usually see others through Somebody

Training vision. Hence, what ordinarily goes through our minds are thoughts from the Lower Self like these:

"Boy, does she wear a lot of makeup! Gross!"

"She'd be beautiful if she didn't have such a big nose."

"Is he ever ugly! Who'd want to go out with him?"

"Is she ever cute! I'd love to take her home with me."

"He's really rude to the cashier. What a jerk!"

"She's such a slob. Why doesn't she make herself more presentable?"

It is now time to change the thoughts you project by picking up an Everybody Training script, one written by the Higher Self. This script is very easy to memorize since it consists of just one line. Now, as you once again find yourself in the midst of humanity, silently say to yourself as you look at **everyone** around you,

I GREET THE LIGHT IN YOU!

"That's it, Susan? I don't even know what it means!" I'll tell you what it means. Within every one of us lives a place of light and love that I have been calling the Higher Self. Perhaps hurtful life experiences have built walls making it invisible. Nevertheless, **the place of light and love is always there!** Projecting the thought **"I GREET THE LIGHT IN YOU!"** allows you to get past the "beautiful" or "ugly" judgment of the other person and to connect with the beauty inside them. Even if he or she seems obnoxious or unfriendly, **"I GREET THE LIGHT IN YOU"** are the words that open our heart and allow us to see beyond the darkness.

And there are other benefits to this ritual. If you see the light in other people instead of the dark, you will automatically experience more light in your life. It makes sense, doesn't it? So from this moment on, no matter how silly it may seem, practice silently projecting the thought, **"I GREET THE LIGHT IN YOU!"** whenever you come in contact with other people. When you are driving your car, walking down the street, or sitting in a restaurant, take a moment to look around you and silently say to each person you see . . .

NO MATTER WHAT I SEE ON THE OUTSIDE, I GREET THE LIGHT IN YOU!

It doesn't matter if this person is a drop-out asking for money or a person of obvious stature and wealth; it doesn't matter if this person is sweet or rude; it doesn't matter if he conforms to our society's definition of attractive or unattractive; it doesn't matter if she is black, white, red, or yellow, or what country she calls home. As we silently greet the light in others, we are projecting our own light into their world . . . and in so doing we are helping to heal not only their pain but our own as well.

A great time to do this exercise is when your patience is being really tried, such as when the cashier is taking a half hour to ring up your merchandise, or when the old man in front of you is driving five miles an hour, or, on a more serious note, when you see someone who is being belligerent or unkind. In the beginning, sending loving thoughts seems frustratingly difficult, but just keep repeating to yourself . . .

NO MATTER WHAT I SEE ON THE OUTSIDE, I GREET THE LIGHT WITHIN YOU!

What you are really saying is "I'm focusing only on the part of you that is wonderful." Aside from bringing our warmth and caring into the world, this kind of thinking:

1. lowers our blood pressure considerably

2. allows us to feel compassion for all other beings, including ourselves

3. brings us into harmony with the flow of human experience instead of creating a block that reduces inner peace

4. puts healing energy into the planet.

Not bad for one little phrase: **I GREET THE LIGHT IN YOU!**

To enhance this process, you might want to imagine yourself projecting from your entire body a healing warm light that envelops everyone you see. You can also project the image of healing warm light into any crowded room. This act will instantly make the room a much friendlier place. I love using the warmth of an imaginary glow to break the ice around people's hearts, including my own.[1]

Another variation of **"I GREET THE LIGHT IN YOU"** is simply to walk down the street, silently (of course!) saying **"I LOVE YOU"** to everyone you see. For those of you who object to the use of **"I LOVE YOU"** except when referring to significant others, remember that we can love at many levels. In this case, I am referring to a love of humanity that includes every human being on the planet . . . yes, even those whom you would like to punch in the face! A friend of mine practiced this for one month and reported a dramatic shift in the way she felt about herself and her relationship to everyone around her. If you live in what is reputed to be an unfriendly city, you will be surprised to see how friendly it seems to become as a result of this exercise. The streets are the most hostile when we build a wall around our hearts.

There are still other variations of this technique. One of my students imagines a heart pinned on everyone's clothes to remind her of the love they carry within them. Metaphysician Stuart Wilde tells us that in order to deal with the negativity around him, he has trained his mind to say the word **"PEACE"** whenever he is in the presence of "strangers." In the beginning, he often forgot and had to remind himself over and over again, but in time this Everybody Training practice became part of his consciousness so that the word **"PEACE"** came through automatically. He says . . .

> By wishing a million people **"PEACE,"** then a million more, you create that energy within you, and gradually what you create is a peaceful world around you. The affirmation becomes real by its constant repetition and by the fact that you really mean it.[2]

These heart-motivated "gimmicks" are reassuring in this world of seeming alienation. They all serve to wake us up to the fact that we are all part of the human family. The ultimate goal is to reach the point where we can no longer look at another person without, at some level, resonating the words **"I LOVE YOU," "I GREET THE LIGHT IN YOU,"** or **"PEACE."**

After you have mastered the art of telepathically greeting the light in others and begin feeling less alienated in the world out there, it's time to up the ante a bit. Now, as you walk down the street greeting the light in others, begin looking briefly in their eyes. You might even want to nod a sign of "hello." I have found in my many years of walking around the streets of New York, Los Angeles, or wherever, that seeing everyone as a "person just like me" makes me feel really comfortable and alive. I smile, nod, and make eye connect with old people, bag ladies, men and women off to work, policemen on the beat, and everyone else I meet.

I know danger sometimes stalks our city streets. Therefore, I don't advise doing this on a deserted street or late at night. Yet, **although it is very necessary to use common sense,** I believe that when we use our "safeguards" of confidence and love, the streets are less dangerous than when we emit an energy of fear or suspicion. Any policeman will confirm that when you have a feeling of strength and belonging, the likelihood of being harmed is greatly diminished. Very often it is when we project our feelings of weakness and separation that we draw trouble into our lives.

There are also many times during the day when you are engaged in face-to-face contact with other people. Begin looking them in the eyes as you speak to them. Start with those that seem the least threatening, such as your bank teller, waiter or waitress, or supermarket checkout person. I don't mean that you should stare at people, nor does eye contact have to be constant. In fact, during conversation our gaze has a natural tendency to wander as we process different information in our minds. But this shouldn't prevent eye contact aimed at perceiving a common humanity: "This is a person just like me."

Remember to **smile** as you look someone in the eyes as it will take away the sense that you are staring. Don't be afraid that they will resent it—most people will welcome your warmth. Dale Carnegie reminds us why dogs are so popular: They go crazy with excitement every time they see you![3] You don't have to go crazy with excitement, but the point is well taken. Take a chance. Start smiling at people throughout the day. Let people know by your demeanor that they're part of the wonderful pot of energy that defines your world.

As you practice this exercise, always remember to replace any negative mental chatter with positive thought projections. They are a *critical* part of the process. As you are passing someone on the street or looking them in the eye, feel the wonder in the fact that . . .

> This is a person just like you, a human being with feelings, who has been rejected at times. This is a person just like you. He (or she) hurts, he feels, he has had many painful experiences, he wants to be liked, he needs approval.

This kind of thought projection will create a far different effect than . . .

> I hope he (or she) doesn't think I'm flirting. I wonder if he thinks I'm a jerk. I wonder why he didn't smile back. I must really be looking like a slob. Maybe I was staring too much, or maybe I wasn't smiling enough.

In this scenario, you focused only on yourself, never on the other person. Instead of moving you to the place of connection, this keeps you in the land of comparison, judgment, and separateness; speaking of which, the following inner thoughts don't work either:

> She's really cute, but such a tacky dresser! Maybe she's a little tall for me. Maybe I should have gone over to the woman standing over there. She seems to have it a little more together.

The kind of energy this creates is hardly a basis for meaningful connection.

Getting back to the crowded room scenario, one question frequently asked in my classes is "What if you approach a person and he or she turns away from you?" My answer is: Never take it personally. Immediately say "stop" to your Chatterbox, which may try to take away your confidence. The truth is that some people may be too nervous to respond in a friendly way. They may only know how to dis-connect. Simply respect their feelings. Turn away, sending them compassion and love. Then try again with the next person.

Another common question is "What if some people mistake my gesture of friendship as a sexual approach?" Some people may indeed misunderstand. If so, simply apologize for the mix-up and explain what's true for you—that friendship was your only aim. (I'll talk more about these two questions in Chapter 6.)

I've also often been asked how we should carry ourselves when facing another person or group of people. My Everybody Training answer to that is simple:

**Walk, sit and stand tall,
delighted that you are who you are!**

There's nothing more you need to know. If you're not feeling particularly pleased with who you are, then simply act as if you were. Say to yourself . . .

**If I were really happy about who I am,
how would I carry myself?**

And then proceed to straighten those shoulders, take a deep breath, and say to yourself at least ten times . . .

I am a pleasure to know.

In this case, let your feelings follow your actions instead of the other way around. It works either way!

A few words about hugs—good old-fashioned body warmth. There's a popular adage in the workshop circuit: "Four hugs a day for survival, eight hugs for maintenance, and twelve hugs for growth." I am a great believer in hugs. I hug as many people as I can during the course of a day. I end business meetings hugging everyone. I hug people at parties that I have met for the first time. I hug my students. I hug my teachers. My husband and I hug constantly. The barriers a hug brings down are enormous!

Self-esteem consultant Jack Canfield tells the story of a man who conducted an experiment to see how many hugs he could give away on the streets of New York. He was startled to find that everyone he asked for a hug gave him one, except one old lady who ran down the street in terror. Bus drivers gave him hugs, policemen gave him hugs, and so on.[4] I guess people are more starved for hugs than we think they are . . . particularly bus drivers and policemen! I don't suggest you conduct this experiment on the streets of a big city, but do take every opportunity you can to hug those around you.

If you are comfortable hugging, you probably don't have to pay attention to your hugging "form." You probably melt into the hug and are not concerned about what part of your anatomy is touching the other person's. If you're not comfortable hugging, your body is probably very rigid; thus you are not deriving any nourishment from the body contact. Focus on relaxing your body. Start from the top of your head and let yourself go all the way down to your toes. The image of melting into the hug is a good one; literally and figuratively defrost and let yourself warm into the other person's being. Again, focus on this thought projection:

I GIVE YOU WARMTH AND COMFORT AS I TAKE IN THE WARMTH AND COMFORT YOU GIVE TO ME. WE ARE TWO HEARTS CONNECTING AS ONE.

This is one exercise that you'll definitely come to love with practice.

For you men out there, get this! Louise Hay reports that St. John's hospital in New York City gives patients who undergo bypass surgery a teddy bear.[5] This is amazing since the majority of these patients are men. The doctors feel it serves two purposes—when a cough comes up, squeezing the teddy keeps the stitches from bursting; and it also provides a feeling of love and security. Hay recommends teddy bears in her work as well. She reports that she has been criticized by a doctor in New York for teaching "infantile behavior" to grown men. Her response is that he was obviously never allowed to have a teddy bear!

Now that you have some help with the "mechanics" of connection, you are ready to stand eyeball to eyeball in front of another person, projecting your warmth and caring. The question now becomes, "What do I say?"

FOCUS ON BEING INTERESTED INSTEAD OF INTERESTING! This means to ask questions instead of trying to impress someone with your wonderfulness. You have probably already noticed that people who go on about themselves can be rather boring! The greatest acknowledgment you can give someone is to be interested in who they are.

Have you ever watched how some people converse at a party? Instead of focusing on the person with whom they are talking, they're busy looking around to see who else is there and to whom they should be talking or would rather be talking! They go through the motion of connecting, but they end up connecting with no one because they're so hung up on making impressions. Impression-making is truly the sad arena of "empty suits."

So, after you introduce yourself, start your conversation with a question and pay attention to the answer.

I'm a salesperson for Red Earth Industries. That's what brings me here. What about you?

I'm a friend of Joe's. How do you know the bride and groom?

I'm your neighbor down the hall. How long have you lived here?

So that you won't be considered an inquisitor, offer some information about yourself as the other person responds to your questions. Even good talk-show interviewers reveal a lot about themselves as they bring forth information from their guests. Very easily, a dialogue will be started.

Instead of the customary question "What do you do?", you might want to start with, "What do you *love* to do?" This offers a better picture of the inside of the person instead of their outer role. It is also a question that will bring forth a more alive kind of energy. Something you love to do is something you can really get excited about. Talking about positive, meaningful things in each other's lives helps to pave the way for a desire to spend more time in each other's company.

Another approach is to offer a compliment. This usually works wonders whether you are in a social or business situation. But make it genuine. Don't tell anyone that you love their intellect when the conversation hasn't gone farther than the weather. Remember that we are not talking about a bag of tricks, but rather heart-felt tools of caring.

You can practice by giving at least ten compliments a day. Really get in to it. Start complimenting people in all phases of your life. We rarely do that. At home, or in the office, or wherever, keep reminding people of their won-derfulness. When I gave this assignment in one of my classes, the feedback was heartening. My students' only lament was that they hadn't learned it earlier in their lives. They couldn't believe how good complimenting others could make them feel about themselves. So begin immedi-ately with those ten compliments a day. Looking at the big picture, there is always something about another person you can genuinely admire.

See how much good feeling you can put out there. Don't withhold any of it. People are fed by your positive vibra-tions. And you'll be fed by the good feelings that are re-turned. **Remember, the purpose of the compliment is not to make them like you, but rather to enrich their lives in some way.**

What we have been talking about throughout this chap-ter is **the language of love**—a Higher Self language most of us are not used to using. Some of it may seem very corny to those of us who are cynical and sarcastic because of past hurts. Many of us may even be embarrassed by the lan-guage of the Higher Self. Notice where your resistance lies. It is only through awareness that change is possible.

Whether or not you are comfortable with the language of love, the lessons to be learned here are not automatic. We have been conditioned over a lifetime to speak **the language of fear.** Expertise in the language of love re-quires practice. I suggest that you first memorize the thought projections, then practice projecting them silently for ten minutes a day when in the presence of others. As you continue to do this, they will eventually become automatic. Then, move forward with the rest of the exercise.

Remember, **never** be upset with yourself when it doesn't go as planned. Like all of us, you are a "lover-in-training," and becoming a lover in the true sense of the word is a life-long process. And, please, **keep a sense of humor about it all.** While these concepts are inherently very important to our well-being, we can all have a great deal of fun learning them if we remember to constantly laugh at our own folly . . . and that of the entire human race!

Just remember this:

People are aching to feel love from us.

This applies even to the passerby in the street. It makes us feel so good to open our heart to others . . . to chat with people any time and almost anywhere . . . to send loving energy as you pass people in the street . . . to remark to someone in a department store that the outfit they're trying on looks great . . . to thank the street cleaner for keeping your city so beautiful . . . to thank the waitress for her great service. On occasion, people will respond hostilely. Make a game out of turning their hostility into love. It takes a lot of determination to keep your heart open and to act friendly when someone is responding negatively. Chances are that your warmth will melt their heart. If not, simply understand that he or she doesn't know any other way to be in this world. What is important is that you do.

I was struck with these words of Ralph Waldo Trine, which were written in 1899:

> The word heaven means harmony. The word hell is
> from the old English "hell," meaning to build a wall
> around, to separate.[6]

While the meanings may differ today, it seems to me that
as we build walls around our heart, we indeed create our
own hell. We separate ourselves from all that is truly beautiful in this world. And what is truly beautiful is the love we
freely give and receive.

Remember that when we become proficient at the
Higher Self form of connection, we become a magnet to
other loving hearts. If we stay stuck in the Lower Self form
of connection, we become a magnet to closed hearts . . .
which is no fun at all! As you allow the reflection of your
Higher Self to permeate your eyes, your smile, your hugs,
your thoughts, and your words, the results will be magical.

6

Some Enchanted Evening

There are many roadblocks to creating a successful relationship, and while we may blame circumstances "out there" for our inability to connect romantically with someone, we would do better to look at some of the beliefs we hold inside.*

From the time we were little boys and girls, our Somebody Training has fed us so many shoulds and shouldn'ts about each other. And as you already have discovered, old habits of thinking and behaving are hard to break. Therefore you may find yourself resisting some of the ideas I will be presenting here. As with anything, use what works for you and let the rest go. Most important, keep an open mind, choosing, wherever possible, on the side of "there are no strangers!"

---

*Don't skip this chapter if you are already in a successful relationship! Most of the concepts can be applied to other areas of your life.

IT ISN'T ABOUT LOOKS!   One of the myths our Somebody Training has taught us is that if we aren't a perfect "10," love will be hard to find. Too many of us are convinced that if we don't meet the right requirements in terms of weight, hair color, teeth, hips, penis length, bust size, no one will love us . . . or we will eventually lose the love we already have! Why are we so quick to buy into the advertisements that are creating these ridiculous assumptions?

All we need to do is to look around and see that finding love has nothing to do with looks!

As an experiment, the next time you walk down the street or go to a party, pay attention to the amazing array of couple combinations that are right before your eyes:

COUPLES IN LOVE

Attractive men with unattractive women

Attractive women with unattractive men

Older men with younger women

Older women with younger men

Older women with older men

Short men with tall women

Short women with tall men

Short men with short women

Fat women with thin men

Fat men with thin women

Women with cellulite with men with firm bodies

Women without cellulite with men who have flabby bodies

Women with gorgeous skin with men whose skin is acned

Men with gorgeous skin with women whose skin is acned

Balding men with women with gorgeous hair

Gray-haired men with gray-haired women

Wrinkled women with unwrinkled men

Wrinkled men with unwrinkled women

Sexy women with unsexy men

Unsexy women with sexy men

And the list goes on!

I'm being silly, but no sillier than most of us are in judging our "lovability" by our appearance. We agonize over our society's definition of physical "flaws" that have nothing to do with finding people to love! Once again we see how our Somebody Training has conditioned us to see people—including ourselves—primarily in terms of externals.

When are we ever going to get it into our heads that looks play a very small part in our ability to create a loving relationship with members of the opposite sex?

As one young man said to me, "Initially looks play a part because that's all I've got to go on. But the minute she opens her mouth, it's a whole new ball game." Yes, initially, we may be drawn to someone because of their looks. But within minutes, or even seconds, other factors enter into the picture. I was once sitting in a cab in New York City waiting for the light to turn green. I looked out the window and saw an incredibly handsome man walking down the street. As I sat there with lustful thoughts roaming through my head, he started ridiculing an old woman who was walking toward him. In one instant, the most amazing transformation took place: this very handsome man turned ugly right before my eyes!

There is a telling line in the story of *The Little Prince*:

> What is essential is invisible to the eye.[1]

When it comes to love, truer words were never written. I look at my wonderful husband and I see only beauty in him, despite the physical flaws he sees in himself. My husband looks at me and sees only beauty, despite the physical flaws that I see in myself. Amazing, when you consider that I have had a mastectomy! Can we be loved if we have only one breast? You bet we can! The other day I was pointing out to my husband a particularly beautiful woman walking down the street. He looked at her for a moment and said, "I don't really find her that attractive. She has one too many breasts!" With that he gave me a big kiss. (No, women out there who may be facing a mastectomy . . . **it's not about breasts!**)

Please **hear** what I am saying. We must stop worrying about the size of our breasts or penises and start paying attention to the size of our hearts! I know our conditioning is pretty hard to resist, especially with the artificial standards of beauty on covers everywhere. But with awareness we can begin to turn our attention inward where it counts, instead of outward where it really doesn't.

To further emphasize this point: How many times have we asked ourselves as we watched a couple walking down the street "What does he see in her?" or "What does she see in him?" Now you know! What they see in each other are those elusive invisible qualities that are essential to a love that works. And what are some of these qualities obviously worth cultivating? Here are a few to begin with:

self-esteem	warmth	caring
aliveness	participation	courage
positiveness	sexuality	confidence
responsibility	authenticity	vulnerability
enthusiasm	vibrancy	humor
passion	strength	lightness
generosity	compassion	empathy
love	kindness	

Did you notice that I haven't said anything about underarm deodorant or makeup or clothes or weight or breasts or skin or whatever other external things upon which we focus too much attention? If you are still not convinced, the best I can do is to leave you with a comforting thought I heard many years ago:

We shouldn't worry about someone judging our bodies because everyone else is too busy worrying about their own!

BE THE KIND OF PERSON YOU WOULD LIKE TO DATE! Interesting notion, isn't it? What do I mean by that? Many negative men and women put in their orders for a positive and emotionally healthy mate. Little do they know that their order is unlikely to be filled! Little do they know that negative energy draws negative energy (and positive energy draws positive energy). What you put out is what you attract. It's really that simple. Hence it stands to reason that

We should all make a list of those characteristics that we would like to see in a potential mate and then GO ABOUT CULTIVATING THEM IN OURSELVES.

It is important to pick up the mirror instead of the magnifying glass, not to judge ourselves, but to determine if we would fill our own requirements in a mate. Are we always complaining? Are we always looking for more, more, more? Are we jealous? Are we fun to be around? Are we out there enjoying all the beauty that life has to offer? Are we angry? Are we judgmental? Are we self-righteous? Do we have a chip on our shoulder? Are we trusting? Are we cultivating those qualities that are "invisible to the eye"?

Another crucial question to ask ourselves is "Are we needy?" Very often we THINK we are very loving people, when we are actually very needy. We "give" purely for the purpose of buying love. We give, not from the openness of our hearts, but because of the neediness caused by our own spiritual separation. And if you think people don't notice, you're absolutely wrong. They do notice and they don't want to be around that kind of negative energy. As you have probably discovered for yourself, there is a smothering quality in a needy person that is very difficult to be around.

If you recognize yourself as needy, what can you do about it? The "cure" is obvious, but it takes time. It is one of those step-by-step processes that we focus on daily. It requires the creation of a rich life, one that includes warm friends, meaningful activities, nourishing time alone, loving contributions to society, and healing relationships with family. In addition, a rich life requires *commitment* to all of the above, knowing that what we do in this life really makes a difference. Those of you who are familiar with my "grid of life" know what I am talking about.[2] To keep neediness out of romance . . .

It's important to have a life that is so full that the absence of romance doesn't wipe us out.

This kind of life defines someone who cares about others, who is involved, who doesn't complain but appreciates the gifts in all things, who listens and reaches out to help others, who respects himself or herself, who has "passion" projects, who appreciates just being alive. None of us would fill all these requirements all of the time; we can learn, however, to fill many of these requirements much of the time.

When you lose your neediness, you become exciting to be around. You feel more powerful. When you walk into that crowded room, you attract emotionally healthy people into your life. And just as important . . .

When you lose your neediness, you also take much of the risk out of love.

Rejection is always a possibility in love. But when your life is so full, the loss of a love will never wipe you out. You may experience sadness, of course, and a temporary hole in your heart, but in a short time, you'll reach out once again, knowing that you have so much love to give to some other beautiful soul. You are, at last, in the blessed position of understanding that no matter what happens relative to a relationship, **YOU'LL HANDLE IT!**

YOUR TYPE IS NOT YOUR TYPE.   If you are not in a successful relationship, the likelihood is that your type is not right for you. You are probably turned on to people who are not compatible and turned off to people who think you are terrific and who would give you loving attention. It is my belief that despite WHY we are attracted to the wrong kind of person (and the reasons are varied), it is possible to see these attractions as **unhealthy tastes that can be changed.**

Let me use an analogy: I used to love my coffee with lots of sugar. That's the way coffee was "attractive" to me. When I decided to give up sugar, I began drinking my coffee without it. It tasted awful, but I persisted until finally I began to enjoy it that way. One day someone accidentally put sugar in my coffee and, you guessed it, it tasted awful! I had totally lost my taste for sugar in my coffee.* Silly analogy, perhaps, but changing my tastes in men happened in much the same way!

The best path of action, of course, is to stick with what we know is healthy for us and avoid that which is hurtful. To judge what's healthy, we should be asking ourselves questions such as:

Does he (or she) support the best of who I am?

Do I feel strong and healthy when I am with him?

Does he seem strong and healthy when around me?

Do I constantly make excuses for him?

Am I constantly trying to change him?

*For you health aficionados out there, don't be alarmed. I've since greatly reduced my intake of coffee, as well!

Is he constantly trying to change me?

Do I feel comfortable being myself when I am around him?

Does he honor his commitments to me?

We need to train ourselves to look at the Everybody Training qualities that have nothing to do with externals, but everything to do with heart and soul. This requires that we hang out with loving partners until it really feels good. I've heard both men and women say after a first date, "He (or she) was really very sweet, kind and loving . . . but I didn't hear any bells ringing." You can guess what I feel about those ringing bells—they're a warning to get your hearing checked!

This is not to say that being sexually attracted to someone is not an important part of a relationship. It certainly is! But . . .

It is far better to allow the sexual attraction to flow from the beauty of an evolving relationship rather than experience an instant attraction that quickly dissolves into disappointment and heartbreak.

While I was not physically attracted to my husband when I first met him, the more the heart and soul within him was revealed to me, the sexier he seemed, until he became—and remains—the most irresistible man around.

So the next time someone approaches you at a party, try looking beyond the externals that have usually attracted you to someone. You might be surprised that the perfect partner for you is nothing like you ever imagined him or her to be. With that thought in mind, it's a good idea not to rule anyone out until you get beyond the nervousness of the first few dates (unless the person is abusive in any way, of course). For better or worse, you might see a very different person emerge from the one that was there on that initial meeting.

A word about age: While a common complaint of women is that men like their women younger, it has been my experience that many men like their women older! Generally speaking, it's not the men who have the problem with older women, it's the women who have the problem with younger men. Why? They feel silly, more conscious of their wrinkles, or threatened by younger women. Hopefully, as younger men with older women become more of an accepted situation, this self-consciousness will disappear.

When it comes to romantic relationships, I don't believe we should make an issue of age one way or the other. People have found love even when extreme differences of age have existed. Who are we to judge how people should or shouldn't find love? Yes, it's true that there are those who choose much older or younger mates for unhealthy reasons, such as to bolster a faltering ego. We should not be judgmental about that either. Such individuals have bought into the Somebody Training curriculum more than others and therefore require external props to prove they are making the grade. If we can see the wounded child beneath the Act, we would have more compassion. But I know from personal experience that it's hard sometimes!

I can't resist telling you of an experience I once had with such a man. I met him at a singles party and up came the subject of age. He told me he was fifty-eight and I told him I was forty-one. He disdainfully responded with "I'd never date a woman over forty." I looked him straight in the eye and lied, "Oh, I know just what you mean. I wouldn't date anyone over forty either!" A look of anguish crept over his face as I excused myself and went merrily on my way. As you can imagine, my Higher Self wasn't too pleased . . . but I must admit, my Lower Self was absolutely delighted!

IT'S PERFECTLY OK FOR WOMEN TO MAKE THE FIRST APPROACH!

I can hear the resistance already, and certainly not from the men! Women, I ask you, Where is it written that men are supposed to be the prime pursuers in the dating and mating game? "But," you are saying . . .

I already tried that and it didn't work!

The men get turned off if women approach them!

Men don't think it's feminine when we're so assertive.

My mother told me never to chase a man.

I understand. When I was younger, I, too, believed that men should do all the approaching. But don't you think that, in today's world, this kind of thinking is glaringly out of place? Here we are, many years after the advent of the women's movement, still choosing to play manipulative games to try to get some man to select us instead of simply walking right up and making the selection ourselves.

I am amazed at the resistance so many women have to the idea of approaching men. They insist that men are really turned off to "forward" women. I put it to the test and asked hundreds of men what they thought about it. And with few exceptions, I learned that . . .

Men love to have women approach them.

In fact, they desperately want women to help them out. They presented some very poignant statements about how it felt to constantly have to make the approach:

Sometimes I feel my heart is breaking.

Some women have treated me very badly when I approached them . . . and it hurts.

I get so nervous that most of the time when I'm interested in someone, I get paralyzed and can't do anything about it.

It's so painful that sometimes I just don't bother.

It's hard. It is something that you want to do and you are afraid of being rejected.

It's like the responsibility is all yours and it really shouldn't be that way.

It's work.

I think it should be a mutual thing. A lot of the time I just end up not doing it. I mean, why should I?

I think that I am more comfortable with it now than I was in high school. But then it was so painful.

We women have to understand that despite how successful, handsome, powerful, adorable, cute, and attractive a man is or is not, the likelihood is that he is just as insecure about approaching a member of the opposite sex as we are. (Once again, we learn, there are no strangers!) The only difference is that our society has, up until recently, demanded that *he* be the one to do it. I suggest, therefore, in the interests of humanity—and equality—we women get in there and help the men out.

**It is cruel and inhuman treatment for men to be the
only ones to put themselves out there to risk rejection. It is also cruel and inhuman treatment for
women not to be able to go after what they want!**

Some women feel it is acceptable to approach a man at
a party, but that making the first phone call is a big no-no.
How did the men feel about that?

I think it's great . . . it's a compliment.

No problem.

I enjoy it.

If a lady doesn't call me, I lose interest. I want to know
she's interested enough to call.

I don't like to always be on the offensive. I really appreciate it when a woman helps out.

Theoretically, I think it would be great. It's never happened. I'm waiting.

It happens too rarely.

One man reported that he met a woman at a party and
they exchanged phone numbers, but he wasn't particularly
interested and probably wouldn't have called her. The next
day she called, and his estimation of her went up 100
percent. He figured she had a lot on the ball to have made
the first move. They dated for quite a long time.

One woman told me that she tried to approach men
twice and she was rejected. This was enough proof to her
that men don't like to be approached. I pointed out that it's
a lucky thing that men don't stop after two rejections, or
there would be very little dating going on! Some men

reported having been rejected by at least *ten* women before one accepted! Psychiatrist David Burns tells us he was constantly rejected. In fact, he calls himself one of the most rejected men in Northern California![3] Oh, the pain of it all! One man suggested that women never have to worry about what to say when they approach a man. "Just say anything. He'll be so relieved that he didn't have to make the approach!"

It is clear to me that something brews beneath the surface that makes women so hesitant about approaching men, and it has little to do with the stated reason that "men don't like it." Let me suggest that what underlies the issue is that **women are frightened of putting themselves in the position of being rejected!** (It is so easy to blame others when we are consciously or unconsciously run by our fears!) Once women realize that it is their fear that stops them from approaching men, not the attitudes of men, they at least know what they have to work on . . . **and it isn't the men!** Their next task is to learn how to "feel the fear and do it anyway!"

You may be asking, if making the first approach is so painful, why would women want to change the conventions of dating? Why not let the men continue to bear the burden of making the initial approach? One good reason is that it removes the need of having to manipulate in order to get what we want. We can let go of all our "drop the handkerchief" tricks and begin acting like our own authentic and more powerful selves. And, even more important, perhaps we'll get what we want—connection!

Before moving on, I don't want to leave you with the idea that all men will like the "new women" approach. Some are still locked in a double-standard mentality. But isn't this an important discovery to be made as quickly as possible? If I approached a man and he put me down for my "forwardness," I would be put off by his "backwardness" and quickly move on to the next person! When anyone puts us down for lovingly asserting who we are, it is our signal to move on to someone else who will love the strength and openness and warmth of who we have become.

There's a very comforting message here for you men out there: **if a woman doesn't approach you, it doesn't necessarily mean that she isn't interested.** It may simply mean that she is too nervous to make the approach! **Don't take it personally.** As you can see, many women have not yet reached the stage where they feel comfortable breaking with tradition and approaching men.

IT NEED NOT BE A BIG DRAMA IF YOUR APPROACH IS "TAKEN THE WRONG WAY"!

As I touched upon earlier, so many women and men express *major* concern over the possibility that someone they approach will assume they're interested only in sex. "What if he thinks I'm easy?" "What if she takes it the wrong way?" In most cases, we have little to worry about. If we are warm and interested, rather than sexual, our approach will rarely be taken the wrong way. But if it is . . . so *what*! As adults, what do we normally do when anyone takes anything the wrong way? **We simply put them straight by explaining how we feel.** And we do this in a caring manner:

> "I'm sorry you took this the wrong way. I'm not interested in sex at this stage of the game. I'd really like to see if we can first be friends."

or

"I'm pleased you find me attractive, but it doesn't feel comfortable for me to become sexually involved with someone I hardly know. Why don't we try being friends and see what happens from there?"

If this is agreeable to the person in front of you, great! If not, great! Once again, you will have discovered very early in the game whether or not this is someone you'd like to spend time with. No harm done. It's really that simple. Why the childlike concern?

I might point out that if your intention *is* sexual, this doesn't make you a bad person. **Nor is someone else a bad person if their primary interest in you is sexual.** That is simply where they are right now in their own personal process of evolving. Why do we assume that someone is putting us down if their interest in us is only physical?* In a sense it is a denial of a very beautiful part of our being, our delicious sexuality.

When I was younger, I was emphatic about the fact that I wanted men to be interested in my mind, not my body. But it certainly doesn't upset me now if someone is interested in my body as well! You see how age matures one! I have no intention of acting on their show of interest, as my marriage is precious to me, but their interest is always reassuring. I'm probably one of the few women who absolutely warms to those construction workers whistling at me. They always get a big smile and a wave in return.

One of the reasons so many women object to sexual

*****Of course,** I am not talking about instances of physical or verbal abuse. Regarding physical abuse, I strongly believe that it is to every woman's advantage to be trained in the art of self-defense. Many such courses are available throughout the country.

advances is that they feel they are being used as sexual objects. I have sad news: As students of Somebody Training, we all have been taught to "use" each other for one reason or another. Men have indeed used women as sex objects . . . and women have indeed used men as success objects. In these changing times, the opposite now applies as well. As we take more responsibility for following the rules of Everybody Training, ultimately our need to use each other as objects will diminish considerably.

By the way, some men report that they come on to women sexually because they believe women expect it . . . and for some women, this is true! For example, I have often heard women complain after several dates if the man hasn't yet made a sexual advance. What is wrong with him? Is he gay? Does he have another girlfriend? Doesn't he find her attractive? They haven't considered the fact he could have been shy, or considerate, or more interested in developing a friendship before jumping into a sexual relationship. It is also true that more and more men are complaining of being used as sexual objects.

The frightening reality of the AIDS epidemic is relevant too. Prior to this universal crisis, whether or not to have sex early in a relationship was purely an emotionally based decision. Now it is a life-and-death issue as well. It demands that great care be taken in choosing someone to go to bed with, as well as what to do when we get there. As with all crises, we need to look at the thread of something positive that the situation offers. Because of AIDS, many of us have discovered a more comfortable new kind of "getting-to-know-you" ritual. We have learned to put more emphasis on friendship rather than sex, which has proved to be a very valuable thing.

For the less courageous among us, it has provided an

acceptable reason to say no. Men have reported that it's taken a lot of pressure off of them to initiate sex when they really aren't ready for it. Women have reported that they feel more comfortable saying no when their health is involved. I know that it is symptomatic of our insecurities that we need excuses to avoid our own truths, but that is simply the way it is at this point in time. The situation will surely improve as we begin having more trust in ourselves.

DON'T TRUST BODY LANGUAGE. Many books have been written about how to read body language, particularly in the area of romance. But knowing what I know about boy meets girl, I question how body language can be read. For example, many women report that they turn away from the men they are most interested in knowing simply because they feel so insecure! Now, in terms of body language, one would assume that if someone turns away from you, they are not interested. Sometimes that is true, but sometimes it obviously is not!

One woman in a singles group reported that she is able to be warm and welcoming with every man in the group except the one who truly interests her. Every time he looks her way, she averts her eyes and turns away, her heart pounding madly. I'm sure the poor man is convinced that he is the only one in the group for whom she has no interest whatsoever! Similarly, one man reported that he can be a wonderful flirt, except with someone he really likes. In that case, he immediately turns away, and too often by the time he regains his composure and turns back again, she's gone. As you can see, it's hard to trust body language when the person who most wants to meet you is the one who is the quickest to turn away from you!

So what's the solution? It's obvious, yet sometimes hard to see.

Go after what YOU want, despite what some-one's body language is telling you. Of course, the risk of rejection is there (and you'll handle that!); on the other hand, you may be pleasantly sur-prised to find someone to love.

STOP TRYING TO BE A MIND READER. "What do women want?" "What do men want?" These frequently asked questions always get an unexpected answer from me:

It doesn't matter what THEY want. Be yourself and see who shows up!

Trying to act the way we think others want us to act is futile. The reason is that everyone has different "wants" in terms of a partner. For example, some men want passive women, others prefer assertive women. Some women want intellectual men, others more physical men. Some people want to be approached assertively, others prefer softer tac-tics. So what's a person to do? Given that everyone has different tastes, it makes sense to **be yourself at all times rather than trying to second-guess the other per-son!**

Simple, isn't it? Yet I watch men and women trying so hard to figure out what the other sex wants and then twisting themselves all out of shape to fit the imagined requirements. And what's the only possible result? **We ultimately learn to hate ourselves (and the other person as well) for not loving and honoring who we truly are.**

Janet, an assertive salesperson, initially acted very passively to the men she dated because she thought that was what they liked. When her assertive nature eventually burst forth after having been cooped up for so long, the men didn't like what they saw. This further reinforced her belief that men like passive women. She hadn't understood the obvious: **If she acted in a passive way, she would draw a man who likes passive women. If she honored her true assertive self and put it out in the world for all to see, she would attract a man who liked her assertive self!**

Janet figured it out when she was spending time with Kevin, a man that she was not really interested in romantically. Because she wasn't that attracted to him, she dropped many of her Acts, not really caring whether he liked who she was or not. Much to her surprise, the more "real" Janet became, the more Kevin was attracted to her. In a short time, Janet discovered what a joy it was to be herself—with all her human strengths and frailties—and to have somebody love all of it! One year later, Janet and Kevin were married.

I can guarantee you that if you honor the essence of who you really are and proudly let it shine through, your chances for a successful "match" are greatly increased. In the end,

> **It's not only about who YOU are attracted to. Equally important is THAT THEY BE ATTRACTED TO THE TRUTH OF WHO YOU ARE! Only in this way can the circle of love be complete.**

With all of the above in mind, here's something to remember when putting our true selves out there in the name of love:

REJECTION ISN'T TO BE TAKEN PERSONALLY.

As I stated earlier, every time we approach someone new,

whether for business, friendship, or romance, we risk rejection, but it seems to hurt most in the area of romance. So, when we approach a potential partner, we have to go into high gear with the important affirmation . . .

NO MATTER HOW THIS PERSON REACTS TO ME, I KNOW I AM A WORTHWHILE PERSON.

If there is rejection, they may be involved with someone else, or prefer redheads, or they could be too nervous to respond to your approach. **Their reason is irrelevant. Your reaction is what's important.** Remember that we cannot control the way anyone acts toward us; we can only control our reactions. Remember, too, that there are lots of other people out there. This is not a "one-drink-of-water-in-the-desert" kind of world. If someone is not interested in getting to know us, there is always someone else who is looking for love.

CONSIDER THIS: If you are constantly getting rejected by potential partners, think of it as an opportunity to look at the "vibes" that you are sending out to other people. Are you sending messages of anger, sarcasm, insensitivity, "walk-over-me" weakness, neediness, or any other message that would turn people off?

All of us in one way or another wear our hearts on our sleeves. And whether our heart is open or closed is revealed very easily to those around us.

If we are sending out positive vibes, as a general rule, we get positive vibes in return. Of course, there are exceptions, but if you are **always** getting rejected, it is a signal that you still have some work to do on yourself. What is important is that you see it as an opportunity for growth, **not as a flaw for which to beat yourself up.**

DO WHAT YOU LOVE TO DO, AND THE DATES WILL FOLLOW!

Where is the best place to meet people? It's not at home waiting for Prince or Princess Charming to show up. It really is necessary for you to put yourself out there where people whom you'd enjoy are likely to be.

The best place to meet people is wherever people congregate to do the things you love to do. And NOT in places where people congregate to do the things you don't love to do.

For example, it is self-defeating to join the Sierra Club to meet someone if you hate the outdoors! You might find a mate, but you may also find yourself covered with the mosquito bites that come with the package! I was once asked if a bar was a good place to meet people. My answer was "Definitely yes, if you love the bar scene and would spend time there anyway. Definitely no, if you hate the bar scene and wouldn't spend time there anyway!"

I am firmly of the belief that "opposites attract" is a misleading statement. In certain personality traits, this may be true. For example, Carol is an assertive woman while Steve is more laid back. This combination of "opposites" works beautifully. But where they are very similarly aligned are in their values and preferred life-style. They enjoy doing the same activities together. This is the very key to harmonious living. Hence, if you do what you love to do, it is more likely that you will meet someone who will also share your values and preferred life-style.

Also keep in mind that a formal setting isn't necessary.

As you practice the techniques in Chapter 5, you'll be able to strike up a conversation in the supermarket, the waiting room at the dentist's office, or on the bus. Seize the opportunity to be friendly. When we are friendly, we meet the nicest people! (**Naturally, take responsibility for attempting this only in conditions that are safe.**)

My suggestion is . . .

> **Do NOTHING in your life for the purpose of meeting someone. Do something simply because you love to do it . . . because it expands the richness of your life . . . because it brings you pleasure.**

When your primary purpose is to meet someone, your expectation is almost guaranteed to reduce your pleasure in the activity itself. And if Prince or Princess Charming is nowhere to be found, you will go home greatly disappointed. So do yourself a favor and take the pressure off by simply following your heart's desire. It is very likely that a person to love will appear when and where you very least expect it.

It is important to understand that the world is filled with people who are looking for love. Don't buy into the articles that tell you that the likelihood of finding someone is next to zero. Look around at the enormous amount of marriages between people of all ages. It can't be as bad as all that!

Even if there were shortages in the available men or women around, the truth is that some people would always find someone great to date and others wouldn't. It has nothing to do with numbers! On a recent lecture tour, I appeared on a television show featuring three women who complained they could never find any decent men to date and three other women who always found great men to date. All six women were physically attractive and successful in their careers. The difference was clearly in those invisible qualities that either attract people or turn them off.

I pointed out the different "vibes" of the two groups of women. The three who had no problems finding great men to date were open, sunny, fun, positive, and obviously really liked people, men included! The other three were sarcastic, judgmental, and carried big chips on their shoulders. It is very clear to me that if the sign on your heart says "Welcome," the love will come pouring in.

DEVELOP A KINDNESS TOWARD MEMBERS OF THE OPPOSITE SEX.

I guarantee that unless you truly think about and treat members of the opposite sex with kindness and respect you're not going to develop a healthy romantic relationship with any one of them. This seems elementary indeed. But the very fact that we have something called "the war between the sexes" is a not-so-subtle clue that for too many of us, a healthy relationship is virtually impossible. One is seldom loving to the enemy!

Many men and women are truly angry with one another, some more openly than others. Each claims good cause for anger. Yes, women, it's true some men will walk all over you. And, yes, men, it's true some women will walk all over you as well. But, in the end . . .

We can't blame anyone for walking all over us. We can only notice that we're not getting out of the way.[4]

It is amazing what happens when we stand tall, take charge of our lives, and act only with integrity toward ourselves. Our lives begin to work and we begin to attract people with the same kind of positive energy. And, contrary to popular opinion, there are plenty of people with positive energy around. But to find them, it is critical that we pick up our mirrors (instead of our magnifying glasses) and work through our anger, lack of trust, judgment, self-righteousness, and neediness, all of which are barriers to loving one another.

The more love we project to members of the opposite sex, the more loving people we will attract. The opposite is true as well. It is only when we finally learn to let go of our anger and open our hearts to each other that we can find wonderful people to love. That's just the way it is.

7

Friendship: The Safety Net of the Heart

My marriage was over. The feeling of emptiness inside of me was hard to ignore. I desperately needed to talk to someone to help ease the pain. I picked up the phone to reach out . . . but I realized there was no one there. And so I discovered at the age of thirty-two after ten years of marriage that I didn't have any friends, not really. While there were many women I cared about and spent a lot of time with, there had never been any authentic sharing between us.

As I listened to Betty's story, I thought back to my own, which was remarkably similar. My first marriage was a time of great activity for me—attending graduate school, raising two children, trying to make a marriage work, entertaining my husband's business contacts, and working part-time. It wasn't as though there weren't people in my life; there were too many! Yet, because I hid so many of my feelings behind my well-defended Act, it was the loneliest time of my life.

I have since learned how to create a deep feeling of bonding with my friends. We have become a source of great love, support, and empowerment to each other. As a result, I now rarely ever feel a sense of loneliness. I have learned to embrace friendship in the gentle and soothing way that Sam Keen embraces it:

> Philia (friendship) seems at first to be the most modest of the modes of love. It is as quiet as a shared cup of tea or glass of beer. . . . It is shared conversation. No howling on the full moon. No demonic explosions of contradictory passions. Friendships make gentlewomen and gentlemen open and unfearful enough to give and receive as a matter of daily intercourse. It lacks romantic trappings, does not demand beautiful partners. Or youth. In fact, it is the solace of those who have nothing else. And when it is strong enough, we need little else—besides bread and shelter.[1]

A beautiful statement about friendship, to be sure. And in this world of constant change and rootlessness, we need the solace of friendship perhaps more than ever before. I have heard it said that friendship may even be more important than romantic love. I am thankful we don't have to make a choice between the two! Both clearly contribute something very special, very different, very important, and very pleasurable to our lives.

It should be noted that there are different levels of friends. First, there are those connected to us only by shared activities. These are the people with whom we study, go to the ballgame, shop, raise our kids, and go hiking, but who do not necessarily share the truth of who we are. Other friends are connected to us only by history. Some go all the way back to our youth and we hold a special place in our hearts for them. The tie of a common background may be there, but the authentic sharing often is not.

Friendships based on shared activities and historical ties are wonderful to have, but **unless they are "deepened,"** they are not enough. What must also be included in our circle of friends are those with whom we can openly and authentically share, heart and soul, the truth of what is going on with us behind our Acts. I'll call these **soulfriendships.** Naturally, if we can create soul-friendships with our activity buddies and our historical buddies, this is great. (A beautiful example of this is given at the end of the chapter.) If not, it is important to look elsewhere.

Soul-friendships are Higher Self friendships, not to be confused with Lower Self friendships, which thrive mostly on shared complaints and commiseration. When people talk about having close friends, very often this is the type they are talking about. While they share their feelings, primarily their anger and hurt, their sharing is usually in the form of blame. Their conversations are characterized by a lot of "Would you believe he [or she] did this to me?" type of questions and a lot of "You poor thing!" type of responses. They become **"complaint buddies,"** and, in that, there is a feeling of great closeness. The problem is that **there is no healing when we buy into each other's victim Acts.** Blaming others makes us powerless; hence, complaint buddies offer only a continuation of our misery. They offer few positive avenues for picking up our power, taking responsibility for our lives, and moving forward with love. That's the bad news.

The good news is that, although filled with negativity, this type of friendship can be considered a step in the right direction. At least it's characterized by an **openness** about anger and pain that is often absent with activity buddies and historical buddies. And if complaint buddies can get off their attitudes of blame, they can often upgrade their friendship from the level of the Lower Self to the Higher Self, thus creating a soul-friendship that ultimately can help us to heal our lives.

Soul-friendships require us to make some major break-throughs: those of us who are closed need to push through our fear of opening up and allow ourselves to be vulnerable to someone else; those of us who constantly complain need to stop blaming and begin taking responsibility for our experiences of life. Not easy! But the benefits of soul-friend-ships are worth the effort and courage it takes to create them. For example . . .

1. SOUL-FRIENDSHIPS ARE THE SAFETY NET OF THE HEART. Despite what happens in our family, business, or love relationships, good friends are always there. And the supply is unlimited! A number of soul-friendships guarantees a shoulder to cry on and a voice to remind us that we need never be alone.

2. SOUL-FRIENDSHIPS PROVIDE THE WELL-SPRING FROM WHICH ALL OTHER RELATION-SHIPS IN OUR LIFE CAN BE NOURISHED. With the help of a rich pool of soul-friendships we can work out our insecurities and fears and gather strength, integrity, clarity, and love. We can then carry out these healing attributes to all our relationships—with parents, mates, children, co-workers, and even the strangers with whom we come into contact every day of our lives.

3. SOUL-FRIENDSHIPS ALLOW US TO KNOW OURSELVES BETTER. In trying to tell our friends who we are and what we are feeling, we explain it to ourselves as well! Good friends also provide a valuable source of feedback; they don't allow us to get away with our Acts. They lovingly demand the truth about who we are. And, most of the time, we take feedback from friends much better than from others, particularly our parents, mates, or children!

4. SOUL-FRIENDSHIPS PROVIDE THE SCHOOL IN WHICH WE LEARN TO LOVE OUR-SELVES (A PREREQUISITE TO LOVING OTH-ERS). Friends are the mirror reflecting the truth of who we are. Through mutual sharing we truly learn that "you are me and I am you." And, by definition, as we cultivate love and compassion for our friends, we cultivate it for ourselves as well.

This last "benefit" brings up the importance of having a number of soul-friendships of the same sex. Same-sex friendships offer an opportunity that cannot be found with members of the opposite sex. That is, they provide a **self-identification** essential for allowing us to see the strength and beauty inherent in being male or female.

When we bond **woman to woman,** we reach deep into the essence of our true (rather than society-imposed) femininity; and when we bond **man to man,** we reach deep into the essence of our true masculinity. It is only then that we find a place that feels like **Home** . . . a place of genuine belonging in the grand scheme of things.

It is here that we touch the power with which our own gender is endowed.

It is here that we stop feeling second-class as men or women.

It is here that we gather self-esteem and begin to feel the awesome contribution we can make as human beings **because of** our sexual identification.

It is here that we can get in touch with a deep, deep level of connectedness that, because of biological and cultural reasons, members of the opposite sex cannot provide for us.

If our friends belong primarily to the opposite sex, it suggests that we are not comfortable with the truth of who we are, genderwise. So many men say they don't like men and prefer the company of women, and vice versa. This is ultimately a harsh putdown of the self.

In order to love ourselves, it is essential that we love our gender as well. It's all part of the package!

Once we feel love for who we are, genderwise, we can then come together—**man and woman**—knowing we have something wonderful to offer each other. This is far more nourishing than coming together humbly praying that some of the beauty and strength of the other person will somehow rub off on us . . . which, if you haven't noticed, is one of the hidden agendas of many men and women interacting together! Hence, we need that time together—man to man and woman to woman—to reflect to each other our inherent value as human beings so that we don't have to beg for it somewhere else.

Psychotherapist Richard Prosapio talks of the value of men interacting with men in order to relate better with women:

It's as if we each have to find ourselves—and we'll be right back. It has to do with standing in the sun for a moment and seeing your own shadow, not blended with someone else's but separate. And then moving out from that place, we (men and women) can come together.[2]

And when we come together from that place of "standing in the sun for a moment," we then have much to learn from each other. Men and women have been conditioned very differently in our Somebody Trained society, and as a result, see the world from very different perspectives, a fact which, in our frustration and insecurity with each other, we often forget. For example, women are trained to be more nurturing, and men to be more success-oriented. As we begin to share our differing "realities," each of our visions widens to take in more and more of the whole. Our Somebody Training, with its emphasis on different roles, taught us to be half people; soul-friendships between men and women can put us on the road to wholeness.

Also, as we share the truth of who we are, we learn to respect one another and to feel compassion for the inner wounds that the "shoulds" and "shouldn'ts" of our Somebody Training has caused both men and women. The pain and insecurity isn't restricted to only one of the sexes as some of us may believe! Along with this feeling of respect and compassion comes the end of the soul-destroying "war between the sexes."

Yes, soul-friendships create incredible richness in our lives. Too many of us, however, don't have a clue as to how to create or participate in a friendship of this kind. Some women are ahead of men in this department. Many have gathered together in groups and learned how to open up to one another. As a result, they have created wonderfully supportive and nourishing soul-friendships. Other women, however, are still enmeshed in the unhealthy "complaint buddy" syndrome I spoke of earlier; that is, they use their friendships to support their complaining. Still others, like most men, are unable to share their deepest feelings with anyone. This means that all of us—both men and women alike—have a lot more to learn about friendship.

With this in mind, it is important to keep reviewing the "essentials of connection" discussed in Chapter 5. The following tips will also help hasten the joyful, yet sometimes frightening, task of forming new friendships and deepening old ones.

First, it is helpful to remember that, aside from the issue of sex, **making friends is very similar to dating.** Think about it!

Just as in dating, there is initial "chemistry" between people which either attracts us or puts us off.

Just as in dating, if we're not picking friends who bring out and support the best in who we are, our "chemistry" is wrong. Our type is not our type!

Just as in dating, our friends are a mirror to our emotional state. If the people we pick are supportive and loving, we're projecting positive self-worth. If the people we pick are negative and pull us down, we're projecting a lack of self-worth.

Just as in dating, it is important to risk rejection and take responsibility for making the first approach. If he or she doesn't seem interested after a few calls, move on to the next person.

Just as in dating, it is important to remember that no matter how anyone acts toward you, you are a worthwhile person.

Just as in dating, there is an initial infatuation period during which your new friend can do no wrong.

Just as in dating, there comes the time when the "honeymoon" is over and you start to see the flaws . . . at which point you either work through the disillusionment and become real friends, or you go your separate ways.

Just as in dating, it is important to be who you are. If someone likes who you are, you have a new friend. If someone doesn't like who you are, no problem—just move on to the next person. Eventually you end up with a friend who wants to be with you **because of** who you truly are, not who you pretend to be or who they want you to be.

Just as in dating, friends can hurt you. With a healthy self-esteem, you pick yourself up and find some new friends.

Just as in dating, the way you make conversation is by being interest*ed* instead of interest*ing*.

Just as in dating, friendships must be cared for and tended, not put on the back burner. They need a commitment behind them. You need to shower them with love. Whether you write a letter, make a phone call, buy a gift, or pay a compliment, it is essential that you let your friends know that they are in your heart. It helps to have an item on your daily calendar, despite how busy you are, that says, "Do something nice for a friend."

Just as in dating, contact with a friend has to be regular. It is important to connect not only in a crisis, but just for the purpose of saying, "Hello, I really care about you."

Just as in dating, it's important to keep working on your self-esteem so you don't become needy. Neediness is a turn-off, no matter what the situation!

Just as in dating, you want to draw friends who build you up instead of diminish you, who help make you feel confident instead of frightened and strong instead of weak, who don't habitually complain but who appreciate the beauty in their lives, who see life's setbacks as opportunities for growth instead of failure, and who can share their emotions.

Now that I've told you some of the similarities between creating friendships and dating, let me tell you an interesting difference. While asking someone for a date is a familiar and readily accepted idea, approaching someone with friendship in mind is often looked upon with suspicion, especially among men. Hence, **creating a friendship for some is more difficult than creating a relationship!**

Part of this suspicion, particularly for men, has to do with fear of being considered a homosexual. And part of it has to do with the **rarity of people reaching out for friendship.** Friendships have taken a backseat in our busy lives. If we have friends, they seem to be acquired through our everyday activities; few of us actually seek friends out.

Potential friends may back away for other reasons as well. For example, along with commitment and intention, soul-friendships also imply responsibility. It's much easier to turn our backs and not care. Hence, it is sometimes necessary to cultivate friendships slowly and with great sensitivity to another's resistance. Remember that becoming part of other people's lives takes time. At the moment, their plates may be full, their schedules crowded. As you keep inviting them into your life, however, they may eventually join you in friendship. Or they may not. Just remember that if someone does not want to include you in his or her circle of friends, the reasons may well not be personal.

For example, my life is extremely full. If I am to honor present commitments to myself, my loved ones, my work, and my community, I am very careful not to overload myself with more people than I can give adequate attention and love. Hence, if I refuse the hand of someone's friendship, it has nothing to do with them personally. It has only to do with my full life.

If you're the one resisting the time and commitment soul-friendships require, it's very important to push through the resistance and make friendship one of your priorities. Friends need to spend blocks of time together—one to one—to nourish the relationship. Short blocks of time rarely allow intimacy to occur. Most of us need a warming-up period to allow us to reach down into real feelings. Initially, we talk about surface happenings in our lives. "Yesterday I did this," or "I just changed jobs," or "My wife hasn't been feeling very well." Only after the stories are out of the way do we get into the deeper levels of our feelings. And it is here that we find our soul-connections with one another.

I have found that one of the easiest ways to get friends to open up to you on a feeling level is for you to open up to them first (and the following chapter introduces you to a great way of learning how to open up). In so doing, you create a safe space for them to come out of their shells. If someone can't handle your openness very well, that's fine. Back off and enjoy them as an activity buddy. More than likely, however, they will respond to your openness by revealing more of themselves.

The greatest benefit that can be derived from our friendships occurs when we help each other to be the best that we can be, as opposed to buying into each other's complaints and feelings of helplessness. So, when friends constantly complain, gently guide them into taking more responsibility for their lives. If the complaints continue, it's time to find some other friends. (You will find that the more positive and loving you become in life, the less you will want to be around friends who are constantly negative.) Don't feel guilty leaving them behind. Remember: they'll always find someone else to complain to!

I want to end this chapter with the voices of three young women who were able to transform their superficial, and sometimes hurtful, relationships into nourishing soul-friendships. The women are Grace, Rachel, and Leslie, "old" college buddies now twenty-nine years old. Aside from their common college experience, their backgrounds are very diverse: three different religions, three different family experiences (one's parents are divorced; one's parents are together but very unhappy; one's parents are happy together, but very repressed); three different economic backgrounds; three different occupations. Each, however, is similarly endowed with a huge amount of enthusiasm, intelligence, and heart.

After being on-and-off friends for eleven years, they decided they wanted their friendship to be more than it was. All three women had begun their own path toward wholeness by attending CODA meetings (as discussed in Chapter 3). This was a great start in helping to upgrade the level of their friendship. To deepen it even further, they decided to make use of a workbook entitled *The Twelve Steps: A Way Out*,[3] which is described as a working guide for people from addictive or dysfunctional families (and we now know that all Somebody Trained families are dysfunctional!).*

The three women committed to meet once a week for six months, each week having completed an agreed-upon section of the workbook. Their time together was spent simply reading what they had written. The reading was not meant to trigger an open discussion. If something was triggered or left incomplete, or if they needed to get some perspective on something, they talked about it. But basically, they were there to share their feelings through their writing.

It is clear to me that their commitment to transform their superficial and sometimes hurtful friendship into a soul-friendship has paid off enormously, as the following excerpts from my interview with them demonstrate:

My first question was "What did your friendships look like earlier?"

Grace: Earlier, I didn't have many female friends. What does that say about myself? That I didn't like myself very much then.

Rachel: I was frightened approaching women. I was afraid of being rejected . . . afraid of being vulnerable.

---

*If you want to use this particular workbook, I suggest you attend a few CODA or other Twelve-Step meetings to first get the sense of what the workbook is asking you to do. Other self-help workbooks are available in the bookstores. Or you can create your own workbook from the exercises presented in any of my books or other self-help books on the market today.

My mother and I weren't very good friends. So I didn't know how to be good friends with another woman. My sisters and I weren't close either. My friendships in school always turned out badly. I remember girlfriends always competing with me, putting on an act. One of them actually created imaginary letters from an imaginary boyfriend. Another one used to say terrible things behind my back . . . that I was drinking, making out, or doing drugs.

Grace: I just didn't value friendships with women a few years back. I never considered myself a good friend . . . because I really burned my girlfriends. When they were no longer useful, I would just disappear. I stopped returning their phone calls. I moved often or found new friends. Perhaps it was a fear of being vulnerable if I got too close.

Also, I didn't choose appropriate people to have friendships with. Part of that was my way of rebelling against my parents. My friendships were also superficial because I never asked for or gave support . . . I didn't think I needed it. I was into being independent. I had to prove I was sufficient on my own. I was enough. A lot of women are seeking independence, and they refuse to ask for help . . . I think it's sad. The only person I needed was a man for things other than friendship. What I realize now is that I *do* need other women—and men—and their friendships. And it's OK to need that. I don't feel weak, I feel strong that I could ask for that.

Leslie: I also used to be superficial in my friendships because I thought if my friends really knew me, they wouldn't want to be around me. I thought I had to be funny, or buy them presents. I didn't think they were there because I had something to offer. I think a lot of the genuineness in our friendships now comes from the growth of our self-esteem.

I asked them to expand on what makes friendships different now.

Grace: For the first time, there is equality. In the past, I was either being helped or helping. There was always a weaker and a stronger person. I find now my friendships are based on mutuality. Sometimes one person is weak and sometimes one is strong, and we help each other.

Leslie: In the beginning, I idolized Rachel, as though she was my big sister. I would go to her with a problem, but I couldn't imagine her coming to me with a problem. I now realize my opinion really matters.

Grace: I can go to my friends now and ask for help. I think that's what's different. We've developed a trust so that when we are in need we can reach out and say, "I need some emotional support right now." "I need you to do something for me right now." "I need you to help me with something right now." I've reached a point where I really welcome that kind of support. It was always there, but I just didn't allow it into my life.

Leslie: I was a very flaky friend. I used to come up with some of the best excuses in the world to get out of commitments with friends. Now my word really means something.

Grace: My ability to form real friendships with women started, I think, with my acceptance that I am a woman. That really bothered me for a long time. I thought women had the short end of the stick, and I wasn't interested in being one. Or doing anything that was feminine. I was very masculine. Now I've learned to value my femininity—my womanhood. And that's made all the difference in the world. I think my initial attitude was a result of looking at the relationship my parents had. My mother was very subservient and my father was the boss. I didn't want to be in her position, but that was the only model I had. Either/or. So I became "Dad," tough and distant. I finally reached a point where I realize that it doesn't have to be either/or anymore. I've gotten far enough away from my family and my home to realize that there are other options. I see different kinds of relationships and other kinds of women. There are dynamics out there that are certainly different than what took place in my home.

Leslie: The three of us have been actively stepping back and getting better perspectives on our families. I'm reaching the point where I am unwilling to be in the dark about what was really going on when I was young and am opening up to the fact that maybe my perception is an illusion . . . or a misinterpretation of what really went on. It pays to look back and say, "Whatever went on, I am no longer going to be a victim of it," then heal the wounds and move on.

Grace: We are all in some way caught up with what we came from. But as adults we can choose not to react and to live a different sort of life. Friends can help each other do that.

Leslie: If I know that something is really off with me and I am reacting inappropriately about something, I can turn to Rachel or Grace and they can pinpoint what it is. I just say, "Something is going on here and I can't see it." And they both know me well enough to know what pushes my buttons. A couple of weeks ago I called Grace and said, "I was really upset with my boyfriend last night and I'm still angry and I don't know what is going on with me." Grace was funny and she was great. She saw exactly what was going on. And we could laugh about it and lighten up about the whole situation. And my anger, which was really inappropriate, went away.

Grace: It gives me great comfort that they are in my life and that I can turn to them when I need to. We were friends before, but at a very superficial and at times dysfunctional level. None of us knew how to ask for help from one another. Even if we felt comfortable doing that, none of us were self-aware enough to know what we needed help for!

Leslie: It's gotten to the point that I can solve problems by just talking to Rachel and Grace in my head. There have been times when I have needed one of them and they weren't around. So I'd say to myself, "If this was their problem and they called me, what would I say?" And the answer comes through, loud and clear. What happens is that I remove myself from the middle of the problem and become my own observer. This takes me immediately out of the heavy drama of the situation. And I can think much more clearly.* I'm learning to trust my own inner wisdom.

Grace: We have learned to tell each other the truth. Sometimes in my writing I would notice myself saying, "I don't want to write that!" And then I'd say to myself, "Who am I hiding it from? It's not like they don't know this. It's not like they haven't felt this." And then I'd go on to expound in great detail on the very thing I was

*You can see this as another version of "lonely me" and "me watching lonely me" discussed in Chapter 4.

hesitant to write about. I'd figure, why am I committing my time and their time and not telling the truth? I'd only be cheating myself. And the more I am willing to risk and the more I am willing to open up, the more I get out of our relationship.

Rachel: When you tell the truth about something, it becomes less frightening. Whatever problem it was for you—your behavior, your guilt, your shame—when you write it down and share it and hear from the other person, "Oh, yes, I've done that before," or "I've felt like that before," then you're able to let it go.

Leslie: When you tell your deepest, darkest secrets and people don't recoil in horror, like you'd think they would, you become healed. There is a personal inventory in the workbook, "a searching and fearless moral inventory of ourselves," and I was really nervous doing it. The instructions are to share it with yourself, God, and one other person. I finally did it with Grace and was really nervous about sharing my truth. What I discovered was that there wasn't anything in my personal inventory that Grace hadn't experienced herself. Beforehand, I had visions of her never calling me again, never seeing me again. It turned out we had so much fun doing it together. And it made us feel even closer.

Grace: I've learned that everything I have ever done in my life, no matter how bad I thought it was, was done to love myself. Sometimes my ideas of loving myself were a bit distorted, but at the base of all my behavior was the motivation to protect myself and find love the best way I knew how.

Leslie: I really cringe at some of my past behavior and feel sad about the part of me that felt that was how I had to behave. Grace helped me to see I had no way of knowing that there was a different way to be. She helped me see that I did what I did because it's what I thought I had to do to get love. It's really helped me have more compassion for that scared, sad little girl inside me who was so needy.

Rachel: What we are doing in this writing group is learning how to forgive ourselves and to love ourselves . . . through supporting each other and supporting our souls. It helps us to say, "Oh yes, I was behaving abominably but I was doing the best I could." And now I can love and forgive myself and act more appropriately. And we laugh about it, which takes a lot of weight off it. For the most part we all identify because all of us have done really ridiculous things.

Leslie: We've also learned to acknowledge the positive changes we see in each other, no matter how minor they may be. We say to each other, "I respect and admire the changes that have been going on in your life." A lot of times you see things that your friend doesn't have much perspective on. Of the three of us, I was the most dependent on men. I did many degrading things just to hang on to a man. I'm very healthy about men right now, and Rachel and Grace constantly reinforce the changes they've seen. I respect the fact that whatever is going on with Grace's life in terms of men, it doesn't affect her self-esteem. She's able to look at it all as a growing experience.

I asked them how, based on their own experiences, people could support each other in a more positive manner.

Leslie: Gently point out the things they do that don't support them, such as sitting around ragging on their boyfriend or their boss or whatever. Gently show them it's not about other people; it's about them. I remember telling someone that, in our group sessions we tell *every-thing,* and he responded, "Boy, your boyfriend must hate that." My boyfriend doesn't have a problem with it at all because we don't sit there and talk about him. It's about *our own behavior.* The best thing you can do for your good friends—if they are willing to have it—is to call them on their "shit."

Rachel: I think friendship is about helping each other find solutions. To point out the positiveness in life, in-stead of indulging in griping.

Another thing we can do to help each other is to de-emphasize the importance of looks. This issue has bothered me for years. I was a model awhile back and I felt like a prostitute because I was doing something I didn't believe in. I was saying, "Buy these shorts and you'll look like me." Well, they wouldn't look like me, and why would they want to? When I finally pulled myself out of modelling, I went to the other extreme. I wouldn't even wear makeup. I gained weight. I didn't care about my hair. Now I've come into a middle ground, where I like the way I look. People who know how I used to look as a model say, "Why don't you dye your hair or wear more makeup?" I always thought of myself as an intelligent woman. Now I look and act like an intelligent woman, and that feels good. I think we are our own enemies when we are so focused on externals. I think we need to reassure each other. I think we have to tell our friends they look great the way they are, and that they *are* great the way they are, regardless of their looks.

Grace: Also, I think friends have to stop each other from putting other people down. When I start talking about other people negatively, I know something is going on within me. I know I need some attention that I am not giving myself. My favorite thought is: If you run into one asshole during the day, well, that's OK. It's a possibility. But if you run into two, it's you that's the asshole . . . and you better look at what's going on inside!

Rachel: We have learned to honor our commitments to other women . . . which is a far cry from the times we would break dates with our girlfriends to be with some guy! When I make a plan with a girlfriend, it's firm, and I wouldn't let her down for anything. My husband is very supportive of that. I encourage him to see his male friends as well. Your mate sees you showing self-respect by honoring your women friends, and he respects you for that—that is, if he is a healthy man.

Leslie: I used to use jealousy and comparison as a way of beating myself over the head. Now I look at what other women have as inspiration, not competition. My first instinct is still "That bitch! Everything is always perfect for her!" The jealousy pops out, but then I quickly jump into "I think that's wonderful. If she has that, it means I can have it, too. There's room for all of us to have what we want." And the thing is that I can now laugh about my bitchiness instead of getting hung up on self-criticism.

Grace: I think your relationships with people reflect how much you value yourself. If you nurture and support your relationships with women, it is a reflection of how you nurture and support yourself. And if you nurture and support your relationships with men, it's a reflection of the same thing. It's *all* the same thing. I'm constantly seeking that special connection with other people. Some people call it seeking God, or seeking a spiritual life, but I'm just seeking a feeling of closeness with other people. When I hit that connection, it makes me feel I really do belong . . . that I have a purpose here.

Three pretty fabulous women, indeed! Their growth warms my heart. To me their story demonstrates what friends can do for our lives that parents and lovers simply cannot. We all need friends. We all need each other.

It is important to recognize that even though there are those among us who are incapable of showing their love for us, that love always exists. The following story that Steve, a corporate lawyer, told me beautifully demonstrates his understanding of how much we all yearn to share our deepest selves.

Jim has been my friend for about twenty-five years. He's very closed and anything I talk about beyond baseball, football, and women he doesn't want to know. But about a year or so ago, he had his third back operation and it was really a difficult situation. Two nights before he had the surgery, his wife called and said he was really down about it. I went over to the hospital where he was already checked in and bought about twenty or thirty bucks' worth of Chinese food and a paper tablecloth and napkins that said "Happy Birthday"—it wasn't his birthday but it was the only kind I could find—and I spread it all over his bed and we had this Chinese food and had a ball. He had his surgery and everything was fine. And he sent me a card. (Now, he's never written a card to me in twenty-five years!) It said, "Dear Steve, I know we have been friends for all these years and I have always wanted to tell you something. I love you and thank you for all you've done for me." I'll save that card till they bury me. Even now when I think about it I get really choked up. Because this is a guy that to this day shows no emotion. So what I think is, this desire to communicate our love is really in everybody. It is really just a question of how you get it out, when you get it out, and who you get it out with.

8

Sharing the Deepest, the Darkest, and the Dirtiest!

Two men's voices, . . . talking about a place where their Acts can be dropped, their masks can be shed, and a sense of belonging is created:

> I don't necessarily come for "enlightenment." I come for camaraderie one night, perhaps to share another night, or to hear someone else share. There is a different kind of energy when you get us together this way, one of membership, belonging, commitment. It's really a marvelous kind of relating that is totally new to me.

> Most men can't say "I love you" to each other. They say it in different ways. I am not someone who communicates well and I have friends who can't communicate well, either, but we have a code. It was the same growing up in my family. The love was there, but it was masked

in jokes or code words. But here, we don't use code
words. We learn to speak honestly and it's safe. The
masks are ripped off. We can cry safely.

Where is this wonderful place where such connection is
possible? It happens to be a men's self-help group, just one
of the growing number of such groups that are cropping up
throughout the country. Women have been coming together in such groups ever since the advent of the modern
women's movement several decades ago. I believe that this
accounts for much of the openness many women have with
each other today. The men are now following suit, and it's
very exciting!

We can build our self-esteem by reading books, listening
to inspirational tapes, and doing our Higher Self exercises.
But it takes human interaction in a safe place to learn the
language of openness which, in a Somebody Trained
world, is a foreign language, indeed!

Too many of us don't have a clue as to what openness
looks like, sounds like, or feels like. We make unsuccessful
attempts at openness and are disheartened by our dismal
failure to connect. As a result, we end up withdrawing even
further into our feelings of alienation. It is in the safety and
support of the group process that we can finally learn the
language of openness in a non-threatening way. We find
out that what we have been hiding beneath our Act is
nothing to be ashamed of; rather, it is wonderfully human.
It is very healing to hear for ourselves that the inner experiences of others are no different than ours.

In the context of the group, we learn with great relief
that we are not bad, or ungrateful, or sick, or alone, or
warped, or lacking. We learn that our feelings are univer-

sally shared. In his seminars, psychologist Ken Druck sometimes asks participants not to reveal their occupations when they introduce themselves. He says . . .

> I was surprised to learn that the inner life of a carpenter is no different from that of a surgeon.[1]

The group process proves that, despite outer differences in our looks, careers, age, financial status, or gender, **feelings are the great connector.** As feelings emerge, the walls of separation come tumbling down and the "empty suits" are soon filled with beautiful human beings.

You may be someone who resists the group process. You may be under the erroneous assumption that people who attend groups are either "crazies" or "losers" who can't make it on their own. On the contrary, they are comprised largely of people who on the surface appear to be making it very successfully. And what motivates them to join a group is the realization that their apparent success has not brought much happiness, fulfillment, or satisfaction. Some are straight business types who have "made the grade," yet know something is missing in their lives; some are newly into parenthood, which brings up many unresolved issues with their own parents; some are frustrated with their inability to communicate with members of the opposite sex. The reasons go on and on. The group provides a safe arena in which they can reveal the truth behind their Acts. Ultimately, they learn to take this truthfulness into the outside world as well—to their mates, friends, children, parents, and workplace.

You may be resisting group participation because you believe that they are attended only by homosexuals. This, too, is untrue. While homosexual men and women have found tremendous value in meeting together in groups to heal their inner wounds, heterosexual men and women are now meeting together in huge numbers for the same purpose.

Or you may be resisting simply because you don't like the idea of opening up in front of a group of "strangers." Underlying your discomfort lies the fear of revealing what you consider bad about yourself. It's an old throwback to the "I don't like airing my dirty laundry in public" mentality, which translates to **"Part of me is dirty."** (That's your Somebody Training talking!)

> **Once you understand the beauty of being "real,"
> you realize there is no such thing as dirty laundry
> when it comes to feelings!**

So if you are resisting the idea of group participation, that's fine. Understand that it's only your fear talking then, once again, "feel the fear and do it anyway!"

This isn't to say that the group process is the only way to learn the language of openness. **There is no ONLY way!** I do believe, however, that it can be the fastest and potentially most joyful. There are many types of groups to explore—therapist-led groups, self-help or self-awareness groups, and the Twelve-Step programs discussed in Chapter 3, to name a few. Each offers a wonderful classroom for learning how to open up—without shame—to the truths we hold within.

Whatever kind of group you may choose, it is important to choose wisely. The important question to ask yourself is: "Is the group based on Everybody Training or Somebody Training principles?" Here are a few guidelines to help you judge for yourself:

An Everybody Training group helps you get in touch with your power. So the question to be asked is, Does the group foster a "victim" mentality or does it help you to take responsibility for your life? If it is a breast-beating scene, with everyone buying into each other's dramas, this is not the group for you.

An Everybody Training group uses such emotions as pain, anger, and loneliness as tools of self-discovery. For example, a "victim" question such as "Why did she do that to me?" would *not* receive a "victim" answer, such as "You poor thing. How could she be so terrible?" The response would be something like this: "What do you think is beneath your feeling of upset?" or "What can you do to stop that from happening again?" In this way, the group's response turns a victim into a creator and in so doing, members of the group help each other to find their own power within.

An Everybody Training group creates pride in your authentic self. If judgment plays a major role in the group, this is not the place for you. This isn't to say that we shouldn't be confronted with our Acts, but in a loving, not critical, manner. Any group that creates more feelings of shame or inadequacy in its members is one to avoid.

An Everybody Training group is not hostile. While hostile emotions, even **verbal** fights, certainly do come up in group settings, it should be a safe place for them to arise. When hostility appears, the group's job is, without judgment, to ask what's really going on beneath all the hostility. It doesn't take sides or pit one person against another. The group is there to serve as a neutral and compassionate observer. And, of course, **PHYSI-**

CAL VIOLENCE IN A GROUP IS NEVER TO BE TOLERATED!

An Everybody Training group is spiritual in nature. The more that we focus on our humanity and compassion in the group, the more we will feel at one with the world around us in our everyday activities.

You will feel awkward as you enter any group for the first time. In any situation involving other people, it takes awhile to feel a sense of belonging. But if, after four or five sessions, you still don't feel very good about being there, or feel abused in any way, trust your gut and try another group.

Given these positive guidelines, the group setting offers a room of **"practice people."** Here, we get to test out the new openness we are learning. Actual soul-friendships may or may not arise from the group. Remember that **friendship is not the purpose of the group;** rather, the purpose is to teach us how to open up, to share, to trust, to learn that we are not alone in our feelings and to feel comfortable with them, to diminish our need to impress others, and to begin to love who we truly are. With this array of powerful teachings, it's then much easier to go out into the "real" world and make those important **one-to-one** connections in all areas of our lives.

In the beginning, there are advantages to attending groups that are same-sexed. What we can learn—men with men and women with women—are:

1. To love our own sex (a surprising number of us don't!).

2. To find our inner power, which many women and men have lost along the way.*

3. To pull ourselves away from the stifling roles that society has placed upon us and discover who and what we truly want to be.

4. To become less dependent on, and therefore more truly loving toward, members of the opposite sex.

5. To get out our anger and grief in a less self-conscious environment.

6. To create a healthy sexual identification (most men have had few male models growing up and most women had models they didn't like very much).

There are a number of areas in which men need greater support than women, and vice versa. The privacy of same-sex groups enables us to work through many of these issues. Here are a few examples (understanding that these issues apply to both sexes but are more pronounced in one sex than the other):

MEN'S ISSUES

One of the biggest barriers to men's openness with each other is the "homosexual taboo." Philosopher Sam Keen points out . . .

> After hearing of the loneliness of men in the course of my many years of leading groups, I have concluded that

*It is my feeling that men's violence toward women represents intense feelings of powerlessness and that the same feelings in women motivate the surprisingly large number of cases of violence against men.

modern men avoid friendship with other men for fear that any tenderness might be a sign of homosexuality. We dare not touch each other, dare not allow the façade to slip, dare not confess that we are vulnerable, lonely, tired, not in control, that our relationships with women have not given us the intimacy we need, that we fear letting loose of our competitive relationships with each other.[2]

This "homosexual taboo" is not as much of an issue for women. Many more women than men feel comfortable walking arm in arm, hugging each other warmly, and crying on each other's shoulders without worrying about accusations of homosexuality. In the safety of a group, men can work through this homosexual taboo.

Another barrier to male friendship is men's intense discomfort in reaching out to one another when support is needed. This discomfort comes primarily from two sources. First, our Somebody Training has taught us that a "real man" can go it alone. And second, men are taught to compete with, not support, one another. As a result, many men suffer alone, which leads to all sorts of soul-destroying addictions, poor health, and even to suicide. Before shooting himself in the head, one man left a note which said simply, "I'm sorry. There is no one to talk to."[3] This in spite of the fact that he was a family man and had three "buddies" with whom he went hunting on a regular basis.

Some men try turning to women for help, but the results can sometimes be very humiliating. While women claim they want open, sensitive men, many (not all) withdraw when feelings they consider weak are actually revealed by their men. It is clear that the need for "the strong, silent type" still exists for many women (as does the need for the "obedient woman" for many men). Our tastes haven't yet caught up with the changing times.[4]

Another source of discomfort that men have in reaching out to other men has historical roots. At the time of the industrial revolution, it was decided that fathers should go off to work and leave the child-raising to the women. Like good soldiers, all the daddies marched out of the house, never to return as intimate companions and teachers to their children. And like good girls, all the mommies went along with the program.

Poet Robert Bly, who leads men's groups across the country, says that, as a result of fathers being absent during their sons' childhoods, a primary emotion in his groups is **grief.**

> Men of all ages . . . look back on their own lives and confront memories of fathers they never really knew.[5]

With no early male intimacy, boys grow up being very uncomfortable with emotion—man to man.

A fourth barrier to male friendships comes from the fact that when their fathers went off to work, men not only grieved for their lost fathers, they also lost touch with their masculinity. This sounds like a strange thing to say in a world where the pressure is on men to get in touch with their feminine side! But it is now being recognized that not only are men out of touch with their feminine side, but they're out of touch with their masculine side as well! This, of course, leaves them in the middle of nowhere.

In the context of a men's group, this lost masculinity can be rediscovered, or at least a newer, healthier model can be created. What men have been portraying up until now with their macho stand is a pseudo-masculinity that has been imposed by a lost society comprised of weak and fearful men and women. Robert Bly suggests that a healthier kind of masculinity looks for "a way to be powerful without being macho and a way to have feelings without feeling feminized."[6]

Given this history, the value of men's groups becomes evident. Here, often for the first time in front of other men, men can allow themselves to cry, to express their feelings of powerlessness and grief, and to be held and comforted. In so doing, they learn to see each other as sources of nurturing and are able to transform their relationships from those of rivalry to those of connection.

You can imagine how powerfully this change of perception can ultimately affect the ability to create soul-friendships outside the group. You can also imagine the relief when men finally realize that they don't have to go it alone. I believe that nowhere can men be shaken out of their intense isolation with more tenderness and compassion than in the "womb" of a loving men's group.

WOMEN'S ISSUES

An important issue to be dealt with in a women's group has to do with the way women's expectations have been created according to the fairy tales they read as children. Men don't seem to buy into these fairy tales as much. Perhaps that is because the Prince Charmings in these pseudo-lovely little stories always seem to get a bum deal! If you notice, they are always cast in the role of heroes (instead of humans) and are usually forced to put themselves at risk rescuing the damsels in distress, who always get to be taken care of. While it doesn't do much for women's self-esteem, it is quite a seductive scenario. Who, at some level of their being—man or woman—doesn't yearn to be taken care of? In a group, women can create a more powerful fairy tale which allows them to feel strong enough to take care of themselves, leaving them less dependent and more loving to men as a result.

Let's take poor old Cinderella as an example: In the original story, we find Cinderella and her stepmother and stepsisters in a terribly dysfunctional and co-dependent relationship. To make matters worse, Cinderella is a classic "victim," totally refusing to take responsibility for her life as she drones day in and day out, "Some day my prince will come."

Enter a manipulative control freak—Cinderella's fairy godmother—who sets up a devious plan to fool the prince. Cinderella, having no backbone whatsoever, goes along with the program and rides off to the ball pretending to be something she definitely is not! Our young prince, fool that he is, is smitten and never looks beyond all the makeup. Cinderella, feeling very insecure (for good reason), disappears at the stroke of midnight, petrified that the prince will find out who she really is!

But never fear. Having delved into his past history, Cinderella's fairy godmother knew that the prince would be drawn to any woman who played really hard to get. Our prince finally finds her via the famous glass slipper, only to discover she isn't quite the person she pretended to be. Nevertheless, he rides off into the sunset with her knowing in his heart that he can change her into anything he wants her to be—and we all know he is right! And if we tune in twenty years later, we find Cinderella sitting around worrying that some young damsel with a smaller foot will lure her "security blanket" away from her. Yuck!

Let's change the story into something much more powerful. How about this scenario? Cinderella goes along with the game plan until she arrives at the ball, when she realizes that what she is doing lacks integrity and she can't go on with the charade any longer. Determined to find a better way to get what she wants out of life, she turns to leave. The prince, smitten by her beauty, runs after her, but she tells him that she isn't ready for marriage; besides, they hardly know one another. She then goes home and packs her little bag, ignoring the guilt trip her stepmother and stepsisters are trying to lay on her. She kisses each one on the cheek, assuring them that they can all make it on their own, and as our tale ends, we see Cinderella walking off into the sunrise to explore all the wonderful adventures life has to offer.

Some of you might prefer my sister's version: After Cinderella's stepmother and stepsisters go off to the ball, Cinderella decides that enough is enough! And she finally takes matters into her own hands. When her fairy godmother shows up and presents her devious plan, mice and all, Cinderella insists, "Forget the prince and get me a locksmith instead!" Since the house originally was left to her by her father, she claims rightful ownership and changes all the locks on the door. Then off to the ball she goes, rags and all, to inform her stepmother and stepsisters that they are no longer welcome in her home. Undaunted by their cries of protest, she turns to leave. The prince, smitten by her fire and spirit, rushes after her, but, knowing his reputation as a spoiled brat, she informs him she isn't interested. "And why are you wearing those funny pants?" she asks. Then she takes off, determined to make a life for herself, and wondering what all those silly women see in him anyway! Back home, she hires an exterminator to get rid of all the mice and begins to redecorate her house the way she always wanted it to be. In the process, she makes a lot of friends, who tell her she's really talented as a decorator and ought to go into the business. And so she does, very successfully. Ultimately she finds a wonderful and supportive male business partner. They fall in love and live happily every after . . . with her maintaining 51 percent of the business.

Yes, a woman's group can help rid us of our soul-destroying fantasies and allow us to explore healthier and much more exciting ways to go forward in life!

Another issue that can be dealt with in a women's group is their unhealthy preoccupation with our appearance. Yes, men are concerned about their looks, but one only needs to glance at women's magazines or listen to their conversations to realize the depth of women's preoccupation with looks. Again, while some women blame men for wanting only those who are "10"s, my experience, professionally and personally, is that men aren't half as concerned about our looks as we are . . . and some don't care at all. With the support of an Everybody Trained women's group, we can begin to understand that a preoccupation with our looks is destructive, and that beauty doesn't make our dreams come true.

A women's group can also help women kick the habit of blaming men for all the ills in the world. Everybody Training teaches that there really are no enemies out there. Clearly, men have been just as badly damaged by our Somebody Trained society as we have—they're just not as vocal about it. In any case, women need to support one another in taking charge of their lives and in not allowing themselves to be taken advantage of. As we realize that we have the power to control our experiences of life, blame comes to serve no purpose . . . and what's left is the love.

A fourth issue for women is a very deep, sometimes

repressed, feeling of being second-class citizens. Many women hide it well with their bravado, righteousness, judgment, and anger, but the deep sense of inferiority that our Somebody Trained society has tried to impose upon them has been clearly felt. As women learn to stand tall with one another, a new dignity and confidence about who they are will ultimately tip the balance. While men also feel inferior, our society is set up in a way that makes it harder for women to feel pride in themselves as a sex. Women can help each other bring forth this self-respect.

Coed groups have advantages as well. Just as having friends of the opposite sex broadens our perspective, so does a mixed group. In fact, in a group situation, you will discover more about the opposite sex than you ever could in a one-to-one friendship. It is here, in a room filled with "practice people," that both sexes feel really safe in opening up. Even in friendship, there is often an image to uphold; hence, openness can be difficult.

If you can't find a self-help group in your area, here's a crash course on starting one.

HOW TO CREATE YOUR OWN SELF-HELP GROUP

1. The first step is obviously to enlist members. Usually, a look through your address book and a few phone calls can start the ball rolling, and friends can help pass the word. You have to decide whether you want the group to be single-sexed or mixed. Each has distinct advantages. The only thing that everyone needs to have in common is an interest in growing as human beings.

2. Create a weekly format. Here is a sample. Remember that nothing is written in stone and you and the other members of the group may find even better ways for creating the environment you want to create. Be flexible.

a. Each member puts his or her name on a slip of paper which is then put into a container. The name that is drawn from the container becomes the leader of the week.

b. The leader of the week reads the statement of purpose that reminds everyone why they are there. For example:

> **We have chosen to be here today for the purpose of reaching out and helping one another to grow into powerful and loving human beings. We commit to coming from that part of ourselves that is filled with integrity and caring. We commit to keeping what is said in this group confidential. We appreciate that we are all human beings doing the very best we can and that through our mutual compassion we can learn to see the light within us all.**

Members of the group can create a circle, hold hands, and close their eyes while the statement of purpose is being read. It is surprising how much "closeness" this circle creates.

c. Begin the "go-around," a warming-up period in which each member has a few minutes to say what has been going on with him or her during the week, or what he or she is feeling at this particular time.

d. Next the leader asks if anyone wants to "work"—that is, to discuss with the group something that is going on in their lives, whether distressing or joyful. The key word is *sharing.* In the early stages of a group's history, much of the talk that may go on is about "story" ("She said to me . . . and I said to her . . ."). But, as the group begins to feel the safety of the room (which could take a long time for some), the feelings behind the stories begin to emerge. Be patient. Opening up, for some very closed people, takes an enormous amount of trust, and some will be able to share more than others.

e. This process is continued for the two or three hours the meeting lasts. Some evenings, not everyone has a chance (or desire) to "work." That's fine. They'll learn from what the others have to say. Eventually everyone understands that "you are me and I am you" . . . and in this way the basis of trust is formed!

f. One variation to get you started is to use the exercises in a self-help book as homework, as suggested in Chapter 7. Then, use the group time to share the issues the assignments bring up. Many of my readers report great success in using the exercises in my books, as the basis of their self-help groups. Many other self-help books contain exercises as well.

Another variation is to have a "theme for the week" for group members to discuss as it relates to their own lives. Some possible themes are loneliness, dependency, anger, friendship, romance, and fear.

g. When the three hours (or whatever time frame the group decided upon) is over, it is wonderful for group members to go around the room thanking each other for being there, preferably with hugs.

h. You may decide to create a system whereby each member is assigned a "growth buddy" in the group, with whom he or she can connect throughout the week to offer support or talk through any problems.

It's helpful to keep to the time limits allotted, as without them, the conversation wanders. Naturally, extra time may be needed if someone is dealing with a heavy issue.

It is important to incorporate the guidelines for an Everybody Trained group as discussed earlier in the chapter. The most important principle is not to fall into a complaining or victim mode of interacting. Rather, the objective is to enable group members to take responsibility for their lives and change what doesn't seem to be working for them.

There are other possible formats. For example, one men's group always starts with a potluck dinner, as they feel that "breaking bread together" helps break the ice. Everyone brings whatever food they want to bring, and sometimes it's a real mishmash, but they don't care. They put it all out on the table with paper plates and cups and for an hour they eat and wind down from the pressures of the day. (Naturally, no alcohol or other drugs are allowed.) Then they're ready to begin.

A few extra tips:

ALLOW ABSOLUTELY NO PHYSICAL VIOLENCE. It is true that conflict often develops in a group session; it's a natural and important part of growth. But this rule must be applied: **If anyone makes an approach toward physical violence, he or she is out of the group.** If verbal conflict becomes too heated, the group leader steps in and mediates. The group can also step in and ask each person involved in the verbal conflict what is really going on beneath the anger. Much personal insight is gained in this way.

DON'T BE UPSET IF SOME MEMBERS DROP OUT. The groups that have been meeting for long periods of time usually have a core group around which other members come and go. Some stay until they've gotten all they can from the group in terms of growth; others, finding it is not for them, leave after one or two meetings. Some group members attend only sporadically. This is also to be expected. As time goes by, you will find your bonding occurs mostly between the regulars.

A GROUP DOESN'T HAVE TO LAST FOREVER. If after a few months a group dissipates, that's fine. Even a short-term experience is valuable, though you may want to join or create another group.

COMMITMENT ALLOWS GREATER GROWTH. Those who get the most out of a group are those who honor its verbal or nonverbal contracts. Commitment means being there regularly, being there on time, and being there when someone needs you. If you show up at meetings only when you need to share a particular problem, that's fine, but true connection comes when you are also there to help others. Otherwise, you never achieve a sense of participation and importance in the human family. It suggests that you don't value yourself enough to feel of value to someone else. And the truth is, you really are important.

DON'T JUDGE HOW OTHERS USE THE GROUP. If you are committed to the group, it may upset you if someone is less so, for example, if they habitually come late or sporadically. Understand that everyone has a different agenda. The key is to take responsibility for yourself and not to judge anyone else. If this is difficult, notice your self-righteousness and work on letting people do what is right for them. Just take the attitude that "Whatever anyone does, it's fine. I'm going to get from and give to whoever is there."

EXPECT AN INITIAL LEARNING PROCESS DURING WHICH ALL DOES NOT GO AS PLANNED.
In a novice group, mistakes are to be expected and learned from. For example, it is scary being the leader for the first time, and the chosen leader may not hold in the reins tightly enough. Members of the group can guide each other and learn from one another. Flexibility is the key. Change what doesn't work and keep the rest.

TAKE RESPONSIBILITY FOR YOUR EXPERIENCES IN A GROUP.
If you don't agree with something, *speak up*. This may be hard in the beginning, but as you feel more comfortable, your courage will increase. Remember that it is helpful to everyone if you tell what is true for you. **Also, if being in the group is bringing up things that are too difficult for you to handle, seek professional help immediately, which leads me to . . .**

SELF-HELP GROUPS ARE NOT THERAPY.
If a group member appears to be embroiled in an emotional problem that is overwhelming, it is important that the group encourage him or her to seek therapy. One man recalled:

> I had a tough time in 'eighty-eight, and it seemed that for a while, everybody in the group was dealing with my depression. I would be silent and the guys would try to

pull me out of it and finally I started to feel ashamed that
I was always depressed. Finally one of the guys said,
"You need more than we can give you. You have to go
to therapy." They made me see that I was using the
group to avoid the real confrontation with my pain that
is best dealt with in therapy. They really pushed me into
getting proper help. And I went to a therapist who pulled
me out of my depression.

You may wonder if therapist-led groups are more valuable than self-help groups. In some ways, yes. A therapist
skilled in the group process can get the group to open up
to each other more quickly. He or she can also avoid some
of the early pitfalls into which a novice group may fall.
Further, a trained therapist is better equipped than group
members to lead the group into meaningful insights. Most
important, contrary to a self-help group, a therapist-led
group can obviously get into the entire realm of therapy,
which can be very valuable. The downside is that therapist-
led groups can be expensive if attended regularly, as they
should be. They are also dependent on the therapist. I
know of self-help groups that have been meeting for over
ten years. Since they have no leaders, they are self-sufficient
and depend only on the willingness of members to show up.

If you decide to try a therapist-led group, it is important
to choose a therapist who leads groups with an Everybody
Trained perspective, as described earlier in the chapter. It
is also helpful when therapists do not portray themselves as
"perfect people," but instead share their own foibles as
well.

While both types of groups—self-help and therapist-
led—differ in a number of respects, I believe that a tremendous amount of value can be gained from both. I have

been a member of both types of groups and they each have played an important role on my journey toward self-discovery, wholeness, and connection.

I also recommend intensive workshops in addition to (not instead of!) an ongoing self-help or therapist-led group. The intensive workshops I have attended lasted anywhere from a week-end to one week. Some are longer. They are usually structured in a way that allows emotional break-throughs to happen within a very short period of time. If you have ever attended weekend workshops, you have watched people arrive with their walls built high, but they very quickly drop their Acts and become real.

Intensive workshops allow us to run the gamut of emotions and are often **verbally** very confrontational in the beginning. But no matter what kind of intensive workshop I've attended, they have always ended up on the kind of loving note that is seldom possible to obtain in our every-day world. I couldn't describe it any better than author and teacher Alan Cohen as he talks rhapsodically about the last evening of a weekend workshop he attended:

By Sunday afternoon something happens, something which I cannot really explain, a rare, even miraculous event that reminds me that life is indeed precious, worth living. It is the merging of twelve half-empty human beings into one whole, living, loving, spiritually endowed Force. It is the birth of the soul into joyous expression, the transformation of Children of God from slumber to aliveness, and the fulfillment of the prayer, "on earth as it is in heaven." I remember one such group of us sitting in our circle on Sunday afternoon, and I tell you it felt as if there was just one big bathtub of love in that room, a universal womb that we all shared.[7]

Yes, well-led intensive workshops are capable of creating a feeling of heaven on earth indeed. I speak from experience. Even if the feeling of sublime connection is only for a brief moment in time, once we have the experience of what is possible in terms of human connection, we are eager to follow the path that leads to a greater opening of our hearts and souls to one another. It feels so good.

Where do you find intensive workshops? They can usually be found in local resource papers. If there is a spiritual bookstore or health food store in your area, announcements of intensive workshops are often posted. The best way of finding an intensive workshop is to mention your desire to attend one to everyone you know. Also, send away to resources that are found at the end of many self-help books. Soon you will be getting announcements of workshops happening all over the place!*

For those of you who are skeptical or frightened about the group process, here are some firsthand accounts. The core of this men's group has been meeting every Thursday night for approximately five years. There are twenty-seven members now, of which ten to fifteen show up at each meeting. Their ages range from the twenties into the sixties. They are all heterosexual. Some are married, some are divorced, some have never been married. Their backgrounds, careers, financial statuses, and personalities differ, but they come together every Thursday night to share an experience that is common to all of them . . . growing up male in our Somebody Trained society. I asked the men to share with you and me what the group has meant to them. Here are some of their answers:

---

*Again, if you are in therapy, consult your therapist if you are planning to attend a self-help group or an intensive workshop.

I have been willing to risk openness with other men because of my experience in the group. The reason for this is that I've really learned here that the bottom line is we're all the same anyway. So, even though someone may be closed to you outside the group, you have to assume that if he were in this group he would be more or less the same. So, I'm much more open out there.

The group really has helped me see *into* a man instead of only looking *at* him. Take Jack. When I first met him I thought, This is one macho guy. Good-looking. A beautiful wife. Corvette. When I got to know Jack better, I realized his macho stuff was a mask, just his way of coping. I've touched enough of his insides to know this is a man who hurts like I do: He can cry; he can feel lonely. So he is no different than the next guy. And if that is the case, then we are all going through this together. And I can relate to the stranger out there in the same way. In this way, I don't feel inferior to someone who appears to have more and I don't feel superior to someone who appears to have less. We're really all the same.

I enjoy being with the guys here. There is a certain freedom. You can tell women many things. I find the women in my life to be nurturing and accepting. But sometimes I really want aggressive, challenging, and honest feedback from a man . . . and that, I get here.

What the group gives me is safety and constructive feedback when I screw up. We have formed an alliance here that feels very comfortable and very strong. I used to be really unsure of myself with other men, but slowly, as I learn to feel more powerful, I'm learning to communicate "out there" as well.

Until I met this group, I relied on women as friends. Now I feel a real bonding with men as well.

The men here are reliable. When I needed help with my house, Tom was there. When I needed personal advice, Al was there. I have another level of friendship with my old college buddies who go back thirty years. When we get together, there is an immediate bonding, but it's based on history, not a sharing of our feelings.

I always had a buddy when I was growing up. After I got married, I stopped the buddy system and my wife became my buddy. After I got divorced women became my buddies. And then one day I realized that I was not cultivating any male friendships. I had gotten out of my male buddy system. And in my own inner journey I recognized I needed some deeper connection with a man or men.

I have never felt a physical connection with men. But here we hug and it feels OK. It's all out of our own bonding together . . . out of our love for each other.

Out in the world, most men will do anything to protect their image. You can't appear vulnerable, and that probably goes back to life in caves sixty-five million years ago. It's only when you get into a group like this that you can leave your image outside and really talk about what you feel and what you are.

When I started to come to this group, I was living with four women—my wife, my daughter, and my wife's two daughters. I really just came for some masculine energy. Sometimes I didn't honestly care what went on, what I said or what I didn't say. I just wanted to be around men because it felt good.

It's still hard for me to reveal a lot of who I am, even though I'm in the group. If I'm not sure of myself, I let it pass. I'm still not comfortable sharing certain things about myself that would make me look like less of a man. But I'm learning.

My parents were very judgmental and expected perfection. I always wondered, "Is there anyone who will accept me as I am?" And then there was Jacob, my first friend ever. We climbed trees, jumped up and down, dug holes, played with marbles and bottle caps, planned a war against the other guys next door, and laughed together. I really loved this guy. Jacob became my link to my genuine self. He was the first person who allowed me integrity and self-acceptance. And this happened at age five. I haven't seen him since I was nine years old and I've never had a friend like that again. This group is the closest I've come.

You know, something has happened to my definition of **strength** since I have been in this group. I used to think macho was strength, but now I realize that it is the courage to open up and be vulnerable. I am in awe when someone has the courage to say, "I am just really feeling sad and naked right now." I think it takes a lot. And I have seen, as some of us have shared at different times, that everybody feels the same thing. They, too, feel embarrassment. They, too, feel shame. And I've learned that one can have all that and still be strong.

I had close friends in high school but not for the fifteen years since. I began to see in this group that really deep relationships were possible in adulthood. As a result, my relationships have become much deeper out there. In fact, I've become "demanding" with those I spend time with. I don't want to hang out with anyone and take time away from my family unless I can have that depth of connection. I've seen what quality is in here, and I want that same quality in other relationships, whether it be with a man or a woman, stockbroker or doctor.

The group has made me realize I am not alone. Other people really feel the same way you do to one degree or another.

I asked how they would describe their relationship with other men in the group. The consensus was:

Friendships are formed in this group, but this is not a friendship group. We respect each other tremendously. We like each other and sometimes we become friends. But a lot of us will never be friends in the usual sense. We won't go out and do things together except on a planned group activity or retreat. I think we connect at a whole different level in here than with "friends" out there. It's more of a "bonding" than a friendship in the traditional sense. And yet I certainly feel that in a moment of need, if I had to get three or four of these guys on the phone, I probably could and I'd probably get the support I need. Yet we might not see each other on a social level.

I asked for any especially significant moments in the group.

We went on a five-day group outing on Jim's ranch in the country. One afternoon, someone suggested we play baseball. All the way from grammar school to high school, I was always the last one to be picked when it came to baseball. Each team tried to push me off onto the other team. I was so ashamed of that. I have been very thankful that as an adult I never had to face baseball again! And here are all my group buddies saying, "Let's play baseball!" I thought, Oh, my God! and voiced my embarrassment to a couple of friends around me, one of whom volunteered to be a team captain. As he opened his mouth to pick his first team member, I heard him call my name first! And it was just so powerful to me. I don't remember if, when, or where I hit the ball, but it didn't matter. I knew their eyes weren't there to judge me. I've carried this experience into so many things in my life. If ever I feel embarrassed or ashamed, I remind myself, "Hey, you're an OK person and it really doesn't matter." And I'm able to let it go. What an incredible impact that day had on me.

What has been very special to me have been the moments we've allowed ourselves to be just silly. I think people in the outside have forgotten or are ashamed of just being silly. For example, during our outing at Jim's ranch, all of us went into the pond and there was nothing but black mud slime on the bottom. I remember Tom started putting mud on everyone and we all joined in. And here we were—a dozen men, all totally covered in this black muck. And we were howling with laughter. God, that felt good.

I think one of the greatest things that happened in a group session was the night where I casually asked everyone to identify their greatest fear, and we went around the room telling our fears. You really had to dig in. I know I was sweating when I was admitting mine. A lot of the guys had the same fears. And a lot of them were different. That was one of the most powerful evenings that I have ever spent.

One of the most amazing evenings for me was the night we talked about homosexuality. Someone started putting down gays and someone else defended them. It was getting kind of heated and someone finally said, "Okay, let's go around the room and each guy tell if he ever had a homosexual thought or experience or not." And then each of us went around the room revealing intimate thoughts or experiences in our childhood and adolescence that could be construed as homosexual. To me that was tremendously revealing about the openness of the group—to admit the truth to a group of heterosexual men and not fear being judged about something like that. I can't imagine a group of men under any circumstances coming forward the way we did with humor, sincerity, and understanding of our earlier experiences, and then simply letting it all go.

One night we went around the room and shared our most degrading sexual experience. When we realized that we all live with nightmares about the ability to perform, it was a big relief.

When I told the group that my father is an alcoholic, that was a real breakthrough for me. I had been grappling with that for years and I don't think I had told anyone else besides my wife. I was stunned when a bunch of the guys said, "Oh, yeah, my father was too." It was such a relief that others had gone through the same thing and we were able to provide each other mutual support.

In the beginning of the group, we heard a lot of words, but not so many feelings. For myself, I remember the evening that I was able to openly express my hurt about something that was going on in my life. That was an important moment for me. It wasn't easily done and it took a lot of trust in myself and everyone here. But it was the first time I could talk to anyone about the hurt I felt inside. I will always be indebted to the group for that.

I had an experience that was so powerful that I have yet to grasp the full significance of it. I joined the group three days after my wife left me. I had not eaten anything or slept since she had left. The group started to chitchat about all sorts of things and I realized I had to talk or I'd explode. I said, "I have to tell you what happened," and I completely broke down. I don't know if the group had ever devoted one whole meeting to one person before. But the whole group was there to help me heal. It was the most incredible thing that I could ever have experienced. Seven months have passed and I've gone from someone who saw absolutely no purpose in living to someone who can now stand up and say that life is great. But what the people here did for me — people who at the time barely knew me — is remarkable. They could feel I was really dying that evening. And that was the night when everybody reached out and didn't let somebody die. So when people in here say, "If I am ever in trouble I know I have people here to help me," God, I know it's true.

These men and the women you heard from in the preceding chapter have already learned one great lesson in life: that their lives make a difference and that they can, by sharing who they are, touch the lives of everyone around them . . . and then some.

9

Welcoming the Heart into the Workplace*

From the lowest job in the hierarchy to the highest, insecurity reigns as we bring into the workplace all the fears of our Somebody Trained childhood.

Am I good enough to make it out here? Is he after my job? What if I get fired? Does the boss like me? Does she make more money than I do? Will I be passed over when the next promotion comes up?

Where there is insecurity, there is competition. Mom and Dad have laid the groundwork long before with "Let's see who can be the first one ready for bed!" In so doing, they unwittingly create a situation where one child ends up

*Remember, don't skip this chapter if you are not a member of the workforce. All the concepts and exercises can be applied to other areas of your life.

feeling smugly triumphant, while the other nurses his or her wounds of defeat. And then we wonder why there is so much sibling rivalry! And so it goes . . . through Little League, school, college, and into the workplace. All our lives we have been given the underlying message, **"BE THE BEST!"**

You may be saying to yourself, "Come now, there's nothing wrong with a little healthy competition." But, as you'll see, it is highly debatable whether such a thing as "healthy" competition even exists.

The alienating wall that is created by competition is evident in all areas of our lives, but it is most visible in the world of work. The reason for this, as Ram Dass points out, is that wherever money and power are key, **everyone,** by definition, becomes a **THEM** rather than an **US!**[1]

If you are the boss, those lower in the hierarchy are a **THEM** because they might steal your job.

If you have a boss, then he or she is a **THEM** because he or she may fire you.

Your colleagues are a **THEM** because they may get ahead of you.

Other companies are a **THEM** because they may steal your business, thereby taking money out of your pocket.

Your friends are a **THEM** because they might become bigger Somebodies than you are.

People of the opposite sex or different ethnic background, age, or appearance, become **THEM** because they may take the job that you feel rightfully should be yours.

Even your family becomes **THEM,** because they don't understand 1) why you are not making more money and/or 2) why you work so many hours and do not spend enough time with them.

How can there be anything but a sense of separateness in such a fearful structure? The question is, "Is it possible to transform the Somebody Training practices, which create separation in the workplace, to the Everybody Training practices, which create connection?"

I strongly believe that we can. In fact, as I look around, I see transformation on its way, like a wave beginning its roll into shore. I don't think we could stop it if we tried! After what seems to have been a very long and very deep sleep, people all over the world are waking up to the fact that our traditional, competitive mode no longer works. Job satisfaction is rare, people consumed with getting ahead are doing so at the expense of personal relationships, and the place we call home—our planet—is being destroyed right before our eyes. Because it's become virtually impossible to avoid all this bad news, people are beginning to take notice, and as a result, a new work ethic is clearly on the horizon. And its central unifying ingredient is clearly **CONNECTION** rather than the every-man-for-himself doctrine that up until now has ruled.

I'd like to suggest some powerful ways that **each and every one of us** can make a difference in helping to make the world of work one of connection rather than competition. I know that one often feels powerless when facing a huge system that seems to be locked into old ways of thinking. Yet there really is much that we, as individuals, can do to create change in our own unique way—whether we are in the mail room or are the Chief Executive Officer of a major corporation, or own our own business; whether we are a teacher, construction worker, lawyer, secretary, or work at home.

I love the following story, told by researcher and author Amy Domini at a business conference held in New York City: A little girl goes out after a storm to throw back some starfish that have become stranded on the beach. Told there are too many starfish for her to make any difference, she says, as she throws one back, "I made a difference to that one, didn't I?"[2] So can you. You will be surprised at how creative you can be when connection (outflow) is the motivation instead of competition (fear), and how you can help turn a dog-eat-dog mentality into an everybody-can-win mentality that will warm the world around you. Here are some guidelines:

EXPAND THE BOTTOM LINE.   The "bottom line" is a very important concept in business, signifying the particular end that justifies ALL the means. If you ask most people to identify what is presently the bottom line in the world of work, they would most likely answer . . .

> GETTING AHEAD!

This, of course, is a shortened version of . . .

GETTING AHEAD (USUALLY AHEAD OF SOME-ONE ELSE!) IN TERMS OF PROFIT, STATUS, AND/OR POWER.

Not great for connection! But what if we did a little mental magic and expanded our bottom line to look like this:

> GETTING AHEAD
> +
> CARING ABOUT CO-WORKERS

As we add a Higher Self dimension to our bottom line, our purpose is greatly expanded. We begin to bridge the gap with our co-workers as we start to see them as people **just like us,** people who would welcome our caring and consideration.

You may ask, "Aren't 'getting ahead' and 'caring about co-workers' conflicting concepts?" Not necessarily. One can be promoted, yet with a sense of humanity instead of smug superiority. The former brings good wishes for success, while the latter brings disdain. Attitude makes a huge difference in our ability to connect with our co-workers.

The actions and attitudes that come from the narrow bottom line of **GETTING AHEAD** are very different from those that come from the expanded bottom line of **GETTING AHEAD + CARING ABOUT CO-WORKERS.** The former strengthens the walls of alienation and the latter strengthen the bonds of connection. **You or me** is soon replaced by **You and me.** With this expansion of our vision, we begin asking ourselves questions such as these:

Am I a positive force in this office (factory, film set, home, or wherever)?

Do I help people feel good about themselves by building them up, or do I pull them down by being judgmental and critical?

Do I offer my help to those who could use it, or do I withhold it, out of fear they may get ahead of me?

Am I a **taker,** or do I also **give** a lot to those around me?

Do I show genuine interest in the lives of my co-workers, or do I act as if I couldn't care less?

As we answer these questions truthfully, we can begin to "correct" into the direction of connection instead of alienation. We can begin doing things that push our loving—instead of competitive—energy out toward the people around us and immediately begin healing the wounds that fear and competition always create. Can you see how this expansion of the bottom line can make the job so much more interesting?

In one of my workshops, I instructed all my students to try expanding the bottom line and participating full-out in their jobs for one entire week. I asked them to act as if their actions really made a difference to everyone around them. The key question they were to ask themselves during the week was . . .

If I were really important here what would I be doing?

And then they were to set about doing it.

Peggy resisted the assignment. She lamented that she hated her job in a public-relations firm and was just biding her time until she found a new one. Each day was pure drudgery as she watched the clock slowly move through the eight painful hours. With great skepticism, she finally agreed to try it for just one week, to expand her bottom line and commit 100 percent to her job, knowing that she really counted.

The following week, as I watched Peggy walk into the room, I couldn't believe the difference in her energy level. With excitement in her voice, she reported the events of her week:

"My first step was to brighten up the dismal office with some plants and posters. I then started to pay attention to the people I work with. If someone seemed unhappy, I asked if there was anything wrong and if I could help. If I went out for coffee, I always asked if there was anything I could bring back for the others. I complimented people. I invited two people for lunch. I told the boss something wonderful about one of my co-workers. (Usually I'm selling **myself!**)

Then I asked myself how I could improve things for the company itself. First I stopped complaining about the job—I realized I was such a nag! I became a self-starter and came up with a few very good ideas which I began implementing. Every day I made a list of things I wanted to accomplish and I set about accomplishing them. I was really surprised by how much I could do in a day when I focused on what I was doing! I also noticed how fast the day goes by when I am involved. I put a sign on my desk that said, "If I were really important here, what would I be doing?" And every time I started to fall back into my old patterns of boredom and complaining, the sign reminded me what I was supposed to be doing. That really helped."

What a difference a simple expansion of the bottom line made in just one short week! It made Peggy feel connected to everyone and everything around her—including the organization itself.

It's important to note that her commitment didn't mean she had to stay at this job forever; it only meant that **while she was there** it was in everyone's best interest, particularly her own, to create a caring environment. Who wants to spend their days in an atmosphere filled with alienation, boredom, and negativity? (I would find it strange if anyone answered "I do!" to that question!) It is also worth noting that with such positive energy, the likelihood of Peggy getting a great recommendation and finding a new, more challenging job would be greatly increased!

Now, let's try expanding the bottom line even further to include still another Higher Self dimension . . .

GETTING AHEAD

+

CARING ABOUT CO-WORKERS

+

CARING ABOUT THE COMMUNITY AND PLANET

Now our actions and attitudes have even more far-reaching and exciting consequences! We now pay attention to the fact that what we do affects the community we serve and the planet on which we live. We now begin to ask ourselves some soul-searching questions, such as:

Am I careless and shoddy in my job performance, thereby possibly causing people "out there" distress and/or harm?

Is the company I am working for (or own) helping humanity or hurting it in any way?

If so, what can I do to change what is not humane?

We now begin considering the **quality** of our work as it relates to the ultimate consumers. We see that what we do makes a difference to someone out there. We also consider the **purpose** of our work and how it affects our planet, realizing we are connected to it all.

The two goals of **GETTING AHEAD** and **CARING ABOUT THE COMMUNITY AND THE PLANET** may conflict. And some changes may be the result. It may require leaving a company that is creating products that we feel are harmful to consumers and the environment. One individual who made such a choice is Don Marrs, who was a very successful vice president of a large advertising firm. But there came a time when he looked around at what he was selling and got a knot in his stomach. He realized that the most exciting and lucrative accounts to work on were cigarettes, soft drinks, cereals with sugar, and oil companies that were irresponsible toward the environment—all accounts that he believed were negative in some way. He talks of the enormous sense of release when he severed his attachments . . .

> I felt an exhilarating sense of freedom from the intolerable weight of having to support values that were no longer my own.[3]

Naturally, it isn't always necessary to change our careers or our companies. A different choice would be to stay where we are and see if a difference could be made from within. But, whatever our choice . . .

When our bottom line is expanded to include our co-workers, the community, and the planet, our sense of alienation is greatly diminished as we realize that we truly are a meaningful part of it all.

Are you beginning to see the advantages?

As we expand the bottom line, we become much more than we thought we were.

As we expand the bottom line, we bring in the human values of **integrity** and **humanity,** which raises our self-esteem.

As we expand the bottom line, the money, status, and power lose some of their initial importance, and fear diminishes as we realize that who we are encompasses more than simply winning the race; it also encompasses our being caring human beings.

As we expand the bottom line, our vision is enlarged to the point where we can see how we are all powerfully connected.

As we expand the bottom line, we become less attached to our roles. We realize that we may be the boss, the secretary, or the clerk in the mail room . . . **BUT WE ARE MORE.** We are all human beings who touch each other's lives.

And as we detach from our roles, the risks are not so great. We don't get so lost in the drama of needing to be important; **WE ALREADY ARE IMPORTANT.** We don't have to prove ourselves to anyone; **WE ALREADY ARE GOOD ENOUGH.** If we lose our job for any reason, we haven't lost our "being-ness"; we know we are much more than our job, so we don't get depressed, scared, and angry (Well, perhaps for a little while!). But then we pull ourselves together and simply move forward in search of our next adventure in the world of work.

We still strive, perhaps even harder, to do our very best, but our attachment to the outcome diminishes. And new, more enlivening priorities step in to replace these limiting attachments. Of course we need money, but . . .

With an expanded bottom line, our identity is not dependent on being the leader of the pack. It is more dependent on how much love we are putting out into this world.

In this light, **GETTING AHEAD** is associated with meaningful connection rather than desperate neediness. So now we have a truly winning formula:

```
GETTING AHEAD
(now with integrity
  and humanity)
      +                          A FEELING OF
CARING ABOUT        =      CONNECTION IN THE
CO-WORKERS                     WORKPLACE
      +
CARING ABOUT THE
COMMUNITY AND
PLANET
```

Naturally, we can continue expanding our bottom line to include more personal dimensions, such as **CREATING MORE BALANCE IN OUR LIVES** and **LOVING THE WORK WE DO.** But in terms of connection, the above winning formula will go a long way toward healing the wounds of separation.

As an exercise, I suggest that you sit down with pen and paper or computer and make three "to do" lists as you answer each of the following questions:

What actions can I take to show my co-workers that I care about them?

What actions can I take to insure that the community and the planet are well-served?

How can I integrate the above with **GETTING AHEAD,** so that it is a win-win situation for everyone?

Take the time to answer these questions in depth. When you think you've gone as far as you can go, think some more; you've only scratched the surface. And when you think you've **really** gone as far as you could go, think some more. You'll be amazed at how creative you can become if you hang in there long enough!

Depending on your situation, you may want to invite some of your co-workers to join with you in this process. Create an evening of sharing your ideas and seeing where you can interact with one another to reach some common goals.

As you begin the task of expanding the bottom line, you may experience a feeling of fear creeping in. Your internal Chatterbox will probably pop up a hundred times to tell you that the dog-eat-dog game is the only way to survive. You can tell that childlike little voice of yours not to worry . . . you're on the right path! The confusion and hesitation will soon pass as you exchange a destructive pattern of alienation and fear for one that is compassionate and life-enhancing.

LEARN SOME OF THE WISDOM OF AIKIDO. It is strange to think of one of the martial arts as a means of connection, but Aikido is extremely healing in its principles. It teaches us about being strong without ever harming someone who is in conflict with us. Aikido has been translated as "the way of blending energy" or "a harmony of spirit and body." Isn't that a wonderful way to begin to look at the world of work?

Three Aikido principles which I find especially meaningful as a way of living from our Higher Self in the world of work (and elsewhere!) are as follows:

1. DON'T FIGHT, DON'T FLEE . . . JUST FLOW.

This means that the alternative to either meeting the enemy with force or simply giving up is to become a channel for the flow of positive energy. A practical way of using this concept is to visualize a stream of energy flowing out from your body that is filled with love, caring, compassion, and connection, particularly when you're confronted with a difficult situation. In so doing you use the **flow** instead of the **fist** to create harmony in the midst of conflict.

When I find myself resisting what's going on around me, and thus blocking any resolution, I imagine myself as a gently rolling sea and let myself physically and mentally relax and flow with the situation. As I do this, I keep silently repeating one of my favorite affirmations:

I LET GO AND TRUST IT'S ALL HAPPENING PERFECTLY.

In a short time, I actually **feel** myself flowing instead of resisting. It is an amazingly powerful way to be in this world.

2. EXTENDING *KI*.

The world of science has discovered that we don't end where our skin does. In fact, a field of energy extends beyond our body and affects everything and everyone around us. Kirlean photography can actually capture this field on film as a body of light surrounding the body. Our physical, mental, and spiritual states determine the "health" of that body of light around our body. It can be negative and limited or positive and expansive.

This energy field is called *ki* in Japan and *chi* in China. Most of us have little understanding of the potential power of our energy field. But powerful it is! For example, when we are positive and expansive, these qualities are radiated out through our physical body into our energy field and we are treated in a far more positive and expansive manner than when our energy flow is negative and constricted. Always remember that energy attracts like energy.

If you look back at the basics of connection in Chapter 5, they can all be seen as an expansion of our *ki*; their purpose is to encompass rather than to alienate those "strangers" in the room. The same can be said of Peggy's new behavior, as described earlier in this chapter. As you learn how to expand your sphere of connectedness, you have a wonderful ability to heal the alienation in the world of work and everywhere else in life. Without it, we tend to remain the victim, who either fights or flees, but never flows.

3. CENTERING. We've seen and heard the phrase **"getting centered"** in recent self-help books and tapes, but what does it really mean? In *Feel the Fear and Do It Anyway*, I showed you how to center by aligning the Higher Self, the conscious and the unconscious mind.[4] In Aikido, centering is similarly defined as the act of achieving balance between body, mind, and soul. If any one of these three components is off balance, life doesn't flow very easily. And it is interesting that by balancing one, such as the physical, the other two are more likely to come into balance as well.

The philosophy and practice of Aikido involve many centering exercises, and again, I invite you to explore them.

It is important for you to understand that . . .

Since we have all been students of the Somebody Training curriculum, we are, by definition, off balance and uncentered!

This is so because we're always looking for external approval instead of focusing on our inner resources. This means that we can be knocked over very easily, literally or figuratively! In addition, we are constantly distorting our very essence by trying to become something other than what we truly are.

When we learn to ground ourselves from within, and when we come from the place of flowing harmony between our body, mind, and soul, there is very little, if anything, that can topple us. We are whole, complete, and at peace, and our vision is clear as we begin seeing through our own eyes instead of those of everyone around us.

Let me give you an example of how I use a version of all three of these concepts—flow, extending *ki*, and centering—when facing what one study reported to be the number one fear in this country—**public speaking.** (In this same study, fear of death was number seven! We'd rather die than make fools out of ourselves!) Are you future public speakers ready?

1. Before I approach the stage, I find a way of looking at the faces in my audience from wherever I am sitting or standing.

2. As I scan the many "strangers" in the audience, I "extend *ki*" by **silently** repeating over and over again, "I love you. I love you. I love you. I love you." I know it sounds corny, but, believe me, as I do this my nervousness begins to melt away and I begin to feel a loving connection with the audience.

3. Once I am introduced, I walk up on the stage and I consciously center myself, "feeling" my feet planted firmly on the ground with roots going down into the earth. As I do this, I visualize myself aligned with my Higher Self and remind myself that my only purpose is to give love.

4. I then imagine a ray of light emerging from above, filling my being with light, and flowing into the room and surrounding everyone sitting before me. These last two steps sound rather time-consuming, but they take only a few seconds.

5. If statements or questions from the audience express disagreement with me, I simply imagine the dialogue as part of the back-and-forth "play" of people learning and growing together—"the way of blending energy." The alternative, rigid defensiveness, only creates alienation and tension in the room.

I cannot describe the high I get when I connect with my audience from that place of love and sharing. This, in contrast, to those days when my knees knocked, my heart pounded, and I was petrified I wouldn't do a good job. Those were the days when I was only concerned about what I was going to **get** . . . such as praise, applause, or a good mark. When I extend my *ki* into my audience now, I am focused on the **giving.** When we are focused on the giving instead of the getting, our fear is transformed into an appreciation for the opportunity of sharing who we are with others.

This simple technique can be used in an interview, a meeting, the office, or anywhere. Yes, even when approaching a bunch of uptight business types walled in by alienation, you can be a healing force by simply projecting an **"I LOVE YOU"** or **"I GREET THE LIGHT IN YOU"** energy into the room. If you can hold on to that loving space, the outcomes of meetings will be very different than when your energy field broadcasts, "I am scared and insecure and I want desperately for you to love and accept **ME!**"

Whenever we approach any situation in a centered state, extending our field of energy and light, we become more powerful and loving . . . rather than fearful and vulnerable.

This is a small taste of the richness of the principles of Aikido. I hope it whets your appetite enough to encourage you to explore further.[5]

TRANSFORM COMPETITION INTO PARTNER-SHIP.

Competition is so inbred in the Western system of business that it is hard to believe that it could be profitable any other way. On the surface, it seems to be true that without competition, there can be no success. But those who have looked a little deeper have come up with a very different conclusion.

In many recent studies, the results surprisingly suggest that the **LESS** competitive one feels, the **MORE** one will succeed! Among other things, competition creates great anxiety and a limited perspective, which diminish performance considerably.

Alfie Kohn wrote a most enlightening book called *No Contest: The Case Against Competition*.[6] In all his extensive research, nowhere was he able to find evidence that competition had value. In fact, he found compelling evidence that

competition is toxic, not only to the job, but also to the soul.
He shows us how competition . . .

poisons relationships,

makes us suspicious, hostile, envious, and contemptuous
of losers,

destroys our self-esteem,

creates anxiety and a need for approval,

is inefficient,

undermines genuine love of learning by focusing on external gain,

and kills curiosity.

He describes competition as an "against-ing" process.
When asked if competition causes aggression, he responds,
"COMPETITION IS AGGRESSION!"[7] He provides
striking evidence that cooperation enhances learning much
more than does competition or an emphasis on individual
achievement, both in school and later in life.

Hence, contrary to public opinion, research is showing
us that competition is *not* the best way to go in business
. . . thereby correcting the myth that the "killer instinct" is
necessary to really succeed in the business world. This is
good news considering that "killers" find it hard to connect
meaningfully with one another. Competition puts people
out of our hearts and makes them objects to conquer instead of people to love.

So what's the alternative? Futurist Riane Eisler suggests
that instead of the Dominator Model, which has prevailed
in recent history, we should look at the Partnership
Model.[8] You may be thinking to yourself, "Partnership is

a lovely idea, but how can it work in the real world, where there is so much conflict?" Yes, conflict certainly does exist. It has always existed and it always will. But conflict doesn't have to be negative. There are ways of transforming it into a source of enrichment and expansion. Up until now, our Somebody Training has taught us to handle conflict in a way that creates **what look like** winners and losers. In truth, **in a competitive system there can only be losers,** because in the process of trying to win, we have . . .

1. created a wall of separation instead of connection

2. lost the opportunity to learn from and integrate into our own thinking other points of view

3. adopted tunnel vision, which shuts out potentially wondrous new alternatives

4. fed our addiction to proving we are better than everyone else

5. caused ourselves to feel more alone in the world

6. closed our hearts to the feelings of others.

I know some of you out there are still saying, "Come now, there's nothing wrong with trying to win. Life would be so dull if there weren't the challenge of competition." This is a common Somebody Training myth. In fact, I'd go so far as to say that most of us are **addicted** to competition. For example, so many of our workaholic tendencies are about being the best, winning, outdoing, proving. The fact that so many people slave away at jobs they don't like, even when they don't need the money, suggests an addiction to winning.

When we are able to let go of this addiction to competition, it is possible to jump to the level of the Higher Self and find an Everybody Training solution to conflict that is far more exciting! Here we can begin to see conflict as opportunity for discovery. What creates conflict are the differing needs, expectations, perceptions, and experiences of everyone involved. If we put all these differences in a big pot and "play" with them long enough, we can come up with some very creative resolutions. In this way, we resolve our differences in an atmosphere of **CO-CREATION** . . . people working together to come up with fresh ideas. Co-creation is much more powerful than competition. It is a win-win activity in an atmosphere of connectedness, expansion, and discovery. The beauty of co-creation is that you don't have to do it alone: it's **YOU AND ME** instead of **YOU OR ME.** What a relief!

Author Merle Shain recounts this wonderful old tale which illustrates the point:[9]

And the Lord said to the Rabbi, "Come, I will show you Hell." They entered a room where a group of people sat around a huge pot of stew. Everyone was famished and desperate. Each held a spoon that reached the pot but each spoon had a handle so long that it could not be used to reach each person's mouth. The suffering was terrible.

"Come, now I will show you Heaven," the Lord said after a while. They entered another room, identical to the first—the pot of stew, the group of people, the same long spoons. But there everyone was happy and nourished.

"I don't understand," said the Rabbi, "Why are they happy here when they were miserable in the other room, and everything was the same?" The Lord smiled. "Ah, but don't you see?" He said. "Here they have learned to feed each other."

In our effort to convert conflict into discovery, expansion, and cooperation, it really helps to see ourselves as beings with very limited vision. By definition, we can see the world through our own eyes . . . and no one else's. That's pretty limited! Conflict simply signifies that those with whom we have disagreements see with different eyes. If we get out of the way of our need to be right long enough to allow ourselves to incorporate their vision into our own, notice how much wider **our** vision becomes:

(LITTLE)	(LITTLE)	(BIGGER!)
MY VISION	YOUR VISION	**OUR VISION!**

I know this is a rather simple model, but it may help you to understand how you are limiting yourself when you have a need to be right and therefore block out the ideas of others.

Understand, **we don't have to end up agreeing with each other.** But in the process, we learn what the world looks like from different points of view. So **LISTEN AND LEARN** is the key to using conflict as discovery. The more we hear and the more we see, the more we allow into our internal computer and the more creative we become—and the more empathy we have for other positions, thus allowing connection to occur.

We are talking about communication . . . and communication is essential in succeeding in the workplace (or anywhere else). Some of the ways to enhance communication in the workplace are:

1. Be open to having your belief systems changed. Each of our beliefs expresses only one point of view. Many others are just as valid. When you are constantly defending something, you can be sure a belief system is controlling the situation. Remember, **a belief system is a wall that separates.**

2. See other points of view as important contributions to the whole picture. Remember the old tale about the blind men describing the elephant? Each saw a different part of the whole. We are all blind men, with the option of expanding our experience and understanding if we listen carefully to others. In this way we incorporate their "truths" into our storehouse of wisdom.

3. Agree to disagree. All differences do not require a resolution. Make your motto, "I can live in my truth and allow you to live in your truth, respecting each of our rights to do so." This facilitates arriving at solutions without anger and self-righteousness. The question then becomes, "You have your belief and I have mine. How can we incorporate both to create a positive solution?"

4. Focus on discovery. For us perfectionists, the concept of discovery rather than achievement is a powerful one indeed. When we focus on discovery, we don't always need to be right; in fact, **it sometimes serves a purpose to be wrong: we may sometimes learn a new way of doing something!**

5. Stop being defensive. If someone appears to "attack" us, whatever the arena, try to move out of the way

of the attack by saying something "disarming," such
as . . .

> I hear what you're saying. Let's see how we can mesh
> our ideas.

> I'm interested in how you came to that conclusion.

> Interesting; I hadn't thought of it that way before . . .

or something to indicate acknowledgment and an effort to
understand the other person. Acknowledgment doesn't
mean acquiescence. It means giving value to the other
person's ideas, even if they differ from yours. Validation of
this sort is a very loving act indeed.

6. Stop criticizing. When we use conflict as discovery,
we no longer have to pretend we know it all. We allow
others to do things their way without passing judgment,
understanding that there can be many pathways to the
same result.

7. Pretend you don't know anything at all. If we
can let go of preconceived ideas just for a moment and
pretend we're ignorant, we're much more receptive to the
ideas of others.

One area in which conflict in the workplace can be seen
as joyous discovery (as opposed to a battlefield) is the interaction between the sexes. At the moment, the interaction
between many men and women in the workplace is still
confusing, confrontive, combative, and certainly competitive. This is not surprising. The roles of men and women
are in the middle of a period of great change. And in a
Somebody Trained world, conflict is the natural result.
Some say that change is not happening fast enough! I

disagree. I feel change is happening at an enormous rate, and if it were happening any faster, the drama would be even more magnified!

Let me remind you that only a few short years ago, women were criticized for choosing to work outside the home. (I know! I was one of them!) Today, many women complain that they are criticized if they choose *not* to work outside the home! Can you understand what this tremendous shift has done to our sense of identity? Even though we are moving in the right direction, toward freedom of choice, an interim period of great confusion is inevitable.

Since conflict is the natural result of even a positive change like this, it behooves all of us to consider it an opportunity for participation and growth, rather than an excuse for hostility. Naturally we have to work consciously to correct any inequities and hurtful behavior that exists. But it is important to understand that men are not the enemy of women, nor women the enemy of men. There are no enemies! There is just change. And during this time of fear and insecurity for both sexes, we need to do all that we can to keep the values of the Higher Self clearly in focus.

What is so important to understand is that **we have so much we can learn from one another.** We must drop the swords and with awe and wonder ask each other to "teach me about this" and "teach me about that." In this way, we will be able to create a dynamic balance that has so far been lacking in the world of work.

The good news is that I see swords dropping and hearts opening already. It is just a matter of time until women, with dignity and self-esteem, will be "holding up half the sky" in the workplace. It is also just a matter of time until men, with dignity and self-esteem, reduce working hours and "hold up half the sky" in the raising of their children.

Then, children will be happier and harmony between the sexes will be restored in a world that has suffered terribly from the destructive Somebody Training practice of polarizing human roles.

Let us commit—men and women together—to creating a kinder new world of connection in the world of work.

WELCOME THE HEART INTO THE WORKPLACE. Ever since women gained the courage to march out of the house and into the workplace, there has been a natural tendency for them to buy into the Dominator Model and act just like men—believing that it was the only way to succeed. Perhaps at one time it was, but times are changing. Faster than we think, the needs of the workplace and the people in it are moving in non-traditional directions.

As discussed in the preceding section, competition, which was the mainstay of the Dominator Model, is now being challenged by more nourishing principles of connection. This shift in direction has enormous implications. Since men have been trained to be experts in competition, **who is the business world turning to in order to learn the principles of connection?** You guessed it— WOMEN!

Journalist Sally Helgesen wrote an eye-opening book entitled *The Female Advantage: Women's Way of Leadership.*[10] One of her reviewers, Tom Peters, said, "Men who wish to stay employed, take heed!" Women in the workplace who are trying to act like men should also take heed!

To understand why women provide what the new world of business needs, we first have to analyze the idealized life-style of the traditional woman. Generally speaking,

- As a child, her games were verbal, fluid, based on cooperation and taking turns.

- As an adult, she was caretaker of hearth and home; competition was relatively absent in her day-to-day dealings.

- She was in charge of creating a nurturing environment and of teaching her children about sharing, caring, and cooperation.

- She mediated conflicts between siblings and other family members in the hope of creating harmonious solutions.

- She was at the center of the activity in the home, unlike her working husband.

- Because of the nature of the home environment and the demands of parenting, she learned to be flexible rather than focused on specific goals.

- In the same vein, she needed to wear many hats to manage all the varied types of tasks the home environment required, rather than becoming an expert in one.

- She often acted intuitively, trusting her own insights instead of what seemed logical.

- She was not only tuned into what was going on within the home, but within the community at large.

- She was rounded in her reading material and general interests in life.

Up until recently, all these characteristics were generally considered liabilities in business. God forbid, whether man or woman, we should ever be accused of acting **just like a woman!** This was not a happy compliment!

Let's now take a look at why these "God forbid" characteristics are becoming desirable in the workplace.

- First, many businesses have become so large that the traditional hierarchy—with the boss alone at the top—no longer works. Instead, the "web," which places the boss in the center of activity, is a far more effective design for accessing information and allowing connection with a larger number of people.

- Because of the information explosion, cooperation and sharing are necessary to prevent important opportunities from falling through the cracks in a world of fast change.

- The need for flexibility, instead of unwavering focus, is also evident in a world where change has speeded up at an unprecedented rate. New ventures crop up overnight and must be acted upon quickly.

- Rather than being locked into roles and singular goals, people in the workforce now need to wear many hats and expand their focus.

- The world is now turning its eyes to the environment, which, by definition, calls for an expanded bottom line that encompasses more values of the heart.

In all areas of the workforce, people's expectations are also changing at an unprecedented rate. Both men and women are demanding work conditions that are nourishing to the human spirit. They're also waking up to the fact that there's more to life than work. Some recent studies indicate that the traditional bottom line—money, status, and promotion—is no longer the biggest motivator for many of today's young. Quality of life—a better sense of balance between job, family, friends, and contribution to society—is taking precedence. What this means is that . . .

> **Companies rigidly adhering to the Dominator Model in which the job comes before everything else are losing their best people to companies that are adopting "feminine values."**

Helgesen interviewed four highly successful female executives and contrasts their business practices with those of traditionally trained men. The women display many similarities to the "feminine" characteristics described above. For example, Anita Roddick, founder of The Body Shop (an international chain of natural cosmetic stores), says that she runs her company on "feminine" principles. What are these principles?

> "caring, making intuitive decisions, not getting hung up on hierarchy, or all those dreadfully boring business-school management ideas; having a sense of work as being part of your life, not separate from it; putting your labor where your love is; being responsible to the world in how you use your profits; recognizing the bottom line should stay at the bottom."[11]

As a reflection of Roddick's commitment to her expanded bottom line, she requires all employees to be involved in community volunteer work—**on company time.** She sees business primarily as a way to help the world . . . not only as a way to get rich.

You may feel that this is all well and good if you own your own company. But what if you work for a large corporation? Nancy Badore, executive director of the Ford Motor Company's Executive Development Center, is responsible for training the company's top two thousand managers worldwide in the values of quality and customer satisfaction, values credited with Ford's comeback in the early Eighties. Under Badore's direction, the company has been shifting from a rigid hierarchical structure organized around competition to a team approach focused on excellence.[12]

Still skeptical? Consider this. Even if a company is not altruistically motivated, it is clearly becoming good business to expand the corporate bottom line from profit to social responsibility. For example, it was just plain good business for Star Kist to be among the first to stop purchasing from fishing companies that are destroying dolphins while catching tuna. It was just plain bad business for Exxon to handle their responsibilities, in the Alaskan oil disaster, in what appeared to be so cursory a manner. One by one, individuals throughout the country and the world are standing up and saying, "No, this is not OK with me," and as their numbers grow, sales are affected.

Understand that the idea of bringing "feminine" values into the workplace is NOT a call to arms between the sexes. In fact, many successful men have always included feminine values throughout their careers. Rather it suggests that we **all**—men and women alike— can benefit from bringing into the workplace those values of the heart that are traditionally assigned to women. I firmly believe that the male of our species will be just as happy to welcome "the feminine way of work" as the women are.

The good news is that it is already happening. In his very hopeful article entitled "Seeking the Soul of Capitalism,"[13] Charles Simpkinson describes a conference of one hundred businesspeople seeking to change soul-destroying business practices. Ben Cohen of the successful Ben and Jerry's

Homemade, Inc., talked about the need for business to be guided by spiritual principles. At the same conference, Mark Albion, a former Harvard Business School marketing professor, talked about the world becoming more economically interconnected and the need for a corresponding increase in interpersonal connections. He spoke of conversations with business executives who had broken down crying because of the intense loneliness they were feeling in their jobs. These same men also lamented the fact that they spent so little time with their families. Many are leaving their high-paying jobs and, in Albion's words, "moving from Wall Street to Main Street."

Change in this dog-eat-dog world is clearly on the horizon, and definitely in the direction of life-enhancing connection. I know change is not easy in a world where competition is a reflex-action. We need constant reminders that there is another way. To help ease you through this transition, I've created the following **EVERYBODY TRAINING ACTION VOCABULARY:**

APPRECIATE	**VALIDATE**	**EMPATHIZE**
PRAISE	**CARE**	**SHARE**
FLOW	**INCLUDE**	**RELATE**
COMPLIMENT	**ENCOURAGE**	**REVEAL**
PLAY	**RELAX**	**BALANCE**
EXPLORE	**COMMIT**	**COOPERATE**
LISTEN	**LEARN**	**GROW**
BLEND	**LIGHTEN UP**	**ENJOY**

As you can see, gone are such Dominator Model words as *compete, win,* and *outdo* that have been so destructive to the human spirit. Keep this new action vocabulary clearly in view during the work-day. It will be a constant reminder of the direction in which to move your behavior. With each step that you take, simply ask yourself . . .

Does this action embody an Everybody Training word or a Somebody Training word?

If the action reflects Somebody Training, adjust your behavior accordingly. For example, if you realize that the action you are taking is one of competing, see how you can change it to one of blending.

I know that for many of you who are heavily involved in the proverbial "rat race," the above sounds a bit naïve. I agree that there is much yet to be done in the workplace and that sometimes our news reports make it seem as though we're moving in the wrong direction. Remember that the media tends to focus on the bad news, in business and everywhere else. As a result, we never get a chance to see all the wonderful transformations that are actually taking place. I ask, simply, that you trust that change is truly possible. More important, trust that **YOU** can be a positive force in the process. No matter what your position in the world of work, remember:

With each act of caring, you contribute to the pool of loving energy that can turn the pointless rat race into a journey of harmonious discovery.

THE SOUL OF
CONNECTION

10

Embracing the World Like a Lover

I believe that it is our nature to connect. Starting from the deepest place within our being and expanding out to our family and friends, the workplace, our community, and ultimately to our entire planet, I believe that we are naturally pulled forward to reach out and touch the entire world around us. I believe that even though our training is about competing, our souls are about embracing. The only thing that stops us are the erroneous teachings of a society that has lost its way.

In the introduction, I told you that *Dare to Connect* contains an element missing in many books of this nature. It's the very same element that's been lacking in our society—which explains very clearly why it has lost its way. As you may have already guessed, I am referring to the element of **spirituality.**

I believe that a society lacking in spirituality offers no

lasting solutions to the problem of alienation that envelopes it. This thought can be very depressing—that is, until we ask ourselves a key question:

Who creates society?

The answer, of course, is

We do . . . you and I.

This reality offers us much hope. It says that you and I can take hold of the reins and begin to steer our society out of the realm of alienation and into a place that feels more like **Home.**

While this sounds like an impossibly difficult task, it really isn't. All that is required is that we begin our own **personal** journey inward to our Higher Self—the best of who we are. In so doing, we play a vital role in the transformation of society at large. As we continue to project healthier thinking and behavior onto the planet, we, along with the countless others who have begun their own spiritual journey, can ultimately tip the scales on the side of love and light.

If you are doubtful that these countless others exist, there is much evidence of a dramatic shift in consciousness all around us. For example, up until recently, the mention of spirituality was strongly discouraged even in self-help books. It was assumed, perhaps correctly, that nobody wanted to read about it. No longer. Books with a spiritual message are hitting best-seller lists throughout the country. This tells us something very encouraging . . .

You and I and millions of others are finally paying attention to the yearning in our hearts for a world bathed in love rather than hate.

Little by little, the spiritual teachings of the few are reaching the hearts and minds of the many. George Bernard Shaw once said that "nothing is as powerful as an idea whose time has come." I believe that the time for a new era of spirituality, hence loving connection, has finally come—and that there is little anyone can do to stop it, even if he or she tried!

While it is still impossible to avoid noticing the many heartless happenings throughout the world, it is also impossible to avoid noticing the many signs of spiritual healing. These signs are everywhere—in medicine, business, religion, psychology, education, politics, and show business. For example, rock stars whose earlier messages were steeped in "sex, drugs, and rock and roll" are now changing their tune. Perhaps the most dramatic television spectacle of the Eighties was Live Aid (created by Bob Geldof and a whole host of other rock stars to feed the starving people of Ethiopia), seen by countless millions of people all over the world and whose theme song was "We Are the World." In medicine we are beginning to see the melding of body, mind, and spirit in doctors' offices and in hospitals where practices such as meditation and the "laying on of hands" are becoming part of the mainstream. A new field of psychology has been created—Transpersonal Psychology—which uses spiritual exercises to heal mental distress. And these are but a few examples.

Spirituality is in the air everywhere. And this fact should offer great hope to those who desperately want to see a society guided by the Everybody Training principles of connection and love rather than the Somebody Training principles of alienation, fear, and competition.

Given that so little formal education as yet relates to the spiritual, we as individuals are faced with a very unique challenge: to find our own way of creating connection where alienation now exists. Here are a few possibilities:

1. We can create connection where alienation now exists . . . by asking the following questions of our Higher Self as we move through each activity of our day and as we touch the lives of those around us:

How can I be softer and more loving here?

How can I reach out to the people in the world around me?

How can I build others up and show them their own magnificence?

How can I expand the bottom line of my entire life and give meaning and purpose to every action that I take?

How can I radiate light in a world that sometimes looks very dark?

How can I open my heart and take more responsibility in healing the hurts I see around me every day of my life?

The questions are never-ending, but without them, we just continue on at our petty pace, healing nothing and perpetuating patterns of pain and loneliness that envelop so much of our world. It is through these poignant questions to our Higher Self that we find answers that nourish us and give us direction.

You've already discovered that in order to actually hear the wisdom of our Higher Self, we need to move the Lower Self out of the way. The incessant negative chatter of our minds is not exactly conducive to great wisdom! Here is where our program of **DAILY** spiritual exercises comes in. As I mentioned earlier, these are available to us through an enormous array of spiritual tools: affirmations, meditation, visualizations, spiritually oriented self-help books and tapes, workshops, and the principles of Aikido, to name only a few.

In doing these healing exercises, we learn how to put spirit into everything we do. **The spiritual is not something out there in never-never land. It is meant to be used in our everyday lives.** The process of putting spirituality in your everyday life is really quite clear:

Ask your Higher Self what is the loving way of doing something, and then follow its instructions . . . NO MATTER HOW MUCH YOUR LOWER SELF OBJECTS!

As we keep repeating this process we begin to drink in the good feelings that loving actions create. Just as important, we create a new kind of life-style (an Everybody Trained kind of life-style) which is infused with love and caring.

Daily exercises allow us to remain conscious about the kind of energy we are sending forth into this world. Awareness is the key. Without it, we fall zombie-like into the Somebody Training habits that create separation. Awareness ultimately allows us to replace these negative actions with the positive actions of connection. And as we thus become spiritually strong, we can't help radiating energy that is a healing force on this planet.

Our daily spiritual exercises also allow us to change our thinking. Teacher Marianne Williamson cites a wonderful line from "A Course in Miracles"[1]:

Every thought leads you straight to Heaven or straight to Hell.[2]

It is clear to me that when we have Somebody Training thoughts of competing, controlling, and comparing, we are led straight to Hell; when we have Everybody Training thoughts about caring, sharing, and loving we are led straight to Heaven. Reflect on your own thoughts and you will see that truer words were never spoken. To change our thoughts requires, once again, that we do our daily homework of replacing the "hellish" words of our internal Chatterbox with the "heavenly" words of the Higher Self.

Spirituality is about our Higher Self . . . the divine within us all. It is about expansion and growth in the direction of love, light, and caring. I believe that touching the world of the spirit is our ultimate human need, the only thing that brings us a sense of wholeness and purpose in life. When we feel those exquisite moments of oneness with those around us, we can be sure we are touching that enchanted world of the spiritual. And when we are in the throes of fear and loneliness, hate and anger, we can be sure that we have lost sight of the spiritual. Therefore, the pilgrimage into the spiritual part of who we are is the most important journey we can ever take.

2. We can create connection where alienation now exists . . . by actually visualizing ourselves projecting light into the world. Again, using the image of light is a wonderful way of radiating out our loving energy to others. Scientists have discovered that people experience much more depression in dark climates than light climates. That makes perfect sense to me. The light of the sun has always symbolized warmth, expansiveness, touching, reaching out. So visualize light pouring forth from every pore of your body as you walk through the world each and every day of your life.

When we project our light onto other beings, we IMMEDIATELY tap into the essence of connection.

3. We can create connection where alienation now exists . . . by seeing ourselves as connected to a Higher Power . . . whatever that means to you. I have heard this Higher Power referred to as many things, such as God, the Life Force, Universal Law, Universal Light, and Christ Consciousness. I seriously doubt that even those of us who consider ourselves atheists have gone through life *never* having felt at least one sublime moment of connection with what appears to be some form of Higher Power. Perhaps we have not identified it as such, but those magical moments of oneness with something bigger than ourselves surely occur . . . for all of us.

When we find a way of connecting our energy with that of a Higher Power, the feeling of being lost in the world vanishes. Again, staying conscious of the presence of a Higher Power requires daily practice, even for devout believers. As I travel around the country giving workshops about fear, I often ask my audiences, "How many of you believe in God?" The room becomes a sea of raised hands. I then ask, "Then why are you afraid?" There is a startled look on most of the faces when they realize that their belief in God is only a belief. They have not as yet embraced God in the center of their being where the seat of trust resides. They realize their journey inward has only just begun.

One of my favorite meditations that gives me the sense of touching a Higher Power is quite simple and very magical in its effect.

a. I close my eyes and take a deep breath.

b. I then imagine myself breathing out *through a large opening at the top of my head* into a vast sky of luminous healing light.

c. Next, I imagine myself breathing in some of this luminous healing light *back through the opening at the top of my head* until it fills up my entire body from head to toe.

d. Finally, I imagine myself breathing out, radiating this Universal Light out into the world through my breath and through every pore in my body, touching everything as far and as wide as my mind can see.

As I repeat this process over and over again, the feeling of a wonderful cyclical connection between a Higher Power, my entire being, and the rest of the world is created. This simple meditation can create a feeling of great peace and power in a very short time.

4. We can create connection where alienation now exists . . . by caring. Caring is another way of projecting light. Acts of caring can be seen as light from the soul. I have seen this light of the soul come forward to touch other souls in many unexpected ways.

One day as I was walking down the street in New York City, I saw halfway down the block a young tough-looking man, his jacket imprinted with a skull and crossbones, swaggering arrogantly in and out of the crowd. I prejudged him as someone who wouldn't give the time of day to anyone on the street—not that anyone would dare to ask! At one point, his eye caught sight of a blind old man with a cane tottering precariously toward the curb. Without thinking, he ran forward and headed the old man off before any damage was done. Then he took off once again. After he progressed a little way, he turned back to see if the old man was keeping on a straight course. No, he was once again headed for the curb. The young man darted back and impatiently told the old man he was still going toward the curb. But to no avail. Yet again, the old man went off course. Finally, with a nod of resignation, our tough guy teamed up with the little old man, and this very unlikely couple proceeded nobly down the street . . . together. Magical! A moment of connection. A moment of the divine. (And an eye-opener to me about judging people by their appearance!)

How easy it is to bring the light of the spirit forth!

One simple act of caring and the whole world is transformed right before our very eyes.

Everyone is touched, uplifted, and comforted. Everyone connects with love. So why are acts of caring not glaringly abundant in our society? There are a few possible answers to this elusive question.

a. To care requires that we keep our hearts open. When our hearts are open, we "feel" the blind man's darkness, the starving child's hunger, the sick woman's pain. For many of us, these feelings are far too painful; we would rather shut them out and not care so much.

But when all is said and done, it is our openness to other people's feelings that allows us to touch the soul within. It allows us to touch our own pain. It allows compassion. It allows a world in which there truly are no strangers.

And, ultimately, we learn that the pain does not wipe us out. It strengthens us. It allows us to walk positively forward knowing that we can learn from all of life's experiences

. . . and so can everyone else, despite what hardships befall them.

b. To care requires responsibility. Many of us don't want this responsibility. We're too preoccupied with Somebody Training ideas of success. We're busy earning a living, rushing through life, wondering when it will all begin to feel good. We don't have time to care. In that, we miss the boat. Thankfully, more boats keep coming back to offer us another opportunity to join the human family . . . and ultimately to understand what feeling good **really** means.

c. To care involves the possibility that someone needs help from us, and many of us don't want to be needed. We don't want to grow up. We haven't yet discovered that it is soul-destroying to remain a child forever. It is only when we finally make the jump into adulthood that we discover the unmatched joy of contributing to someone else's life in our own unique way.

One dilemma we all face when we finally do grow up is that there is so much caring to be done in the world! How do we cope with it all? We begin by understanding that **we don't have to do it all.** We take it one step at a time, acting only on those situations that intuitively pull us in their direction and letting the rest go, trusting that others will be there to say "yes" where we have said "no."

d. To care requires giving the gift of ourselves, and some of us feel we have nothing to offer. How much opportunity for connecting we miss by thinking such a powerless thought! We all have something to offer, whatever our circumstances.

I knew of a woman in New York who was confined to her bed. What did she have to offer? She asked her Higher

Self the same question and came up with a wonderful answer. She had a telephone and she still had a voice. Through a social service agency, she obtained a list of other bedridden people, and spent most of her waking hours calling these people just to let them know that somebody cared. Many of them became her "telephone buddies."

It takes so little . . . just a little attention off the self, the opportunity to say to someone else, "Hi, I'm here. How can I help you on your journey on this very strange planet?"

To care is to automatically become at one with another soul.

We can bring a quality of caring to all our human exchanges, whatever they may be. We innately thirst for the feelings that come from acts of caring. They make us feel useful, connected, and spiritually whole. Acts of caring make life worth living. A life of emptiness could be transformed by a life of caring.

5. We can create connection where alienation now exists . . . by creating a feeling of family with the world of "strangers" around us. With today's Somebody Training focus on materialism, success, and getting ahead we have lost the comfort that a sense of family can bring.

One way of enhancing the feeling of family around us is to stop the **us-versus-them** mentality that pervades our Somebody Trained society. We need to stay conscious when politicians talk about **them,** when the media talks about **them,** when our friends and family talk about **them.** We need to stay conscious when we hear statements such as "Why should we feed people over there when there are people starving over here?"

In a world where there are no strangers, there is no "over there." There is only all of us . . . everywhere . . . one human family!

One of the most poignant expressions of this philosophy was made by Tony Benn, an English parliamentarian, as young men were being brought home from the Falkland Islands war in coffins draped with the British flag. He said . . .

"We can't kill over flags any more."

No, we can't, not if we hope to achieve spiritual wholeness and survive as a planet. Nothing is so damaging to our inner sense of connection as an **us-versus-them** kind of message. We need to be constantly on watch so that a new kind of thinking can be brought forth onto this planet . . . the kind of thinking that creates only connection and love. And as we begin to look deep inside, we notice that all our longing pulls us in that direction.

6. We can create connection where alienation now exists . . . by committing to something about which we feel very deeply—the environment, literacy, hunger, peace, or a community project—knowing that we are important members of this global family. If you don't *believe* that you are important, *act* as if you are. This is one of the few times when "acting" is permissable. Ask yourself . . .

If I were really an important member of this global family, what would I be doing?

And then proceed to *do* it one step at a time. You will be amazed at how much distance your loving light can cover in this step-by-step process.

7. We can create connection where alienation now exists . . . by making our spiritual growth a life-long commitment. Yes, it does take that long . . . perhaps longer! I know of no one who has yet achieved 100 percent enlightenment. Even our great spiritual teachers continually laugh at their own lapses into the realm of the ego or Lower Self. They, too, have the need to monitor their thoughts, words, and behavior **DAILY.** Once again we see that "there are no strangers," even among our greatest teachers.

Learning the art of patience is part of our spiritual journey. The world does not change overnight, nor do we. For all of us, it is a constant process of learning and growing. It is a process of using all life experiences to show us the way Home. **And with each step forward, we come closer to the truth of our own magnificence.**

The road to connection is clear. It begins inside and radiates out to everyone around us in an ever-growing beam of light. Perhaps it will help make those first few steps of the journey easier, when we understand that creating a feeling of connection, first with ourselves and then with others, is perhaps the most important thing we can do for ourselves.

Rabbi Harold Kushner was watching two children building sand castles at the water's edge. Just when they had finished an elaborate castle that took much time and patience, a wave came along and knocked it down. He expected tears and upset. Instead they sat there laughing and holding hands and soon began building another castle. He said,

I realized that they had taught me an important lesson. All the things in our lives, all the complicated structures we spend so much time and energy creating, are built on sand. Only our relationships to other people endure. Sooner or later, the wave will come along and knock down what we have worked so hard to build up. When that happens, only the person who has somebody's hand to hold will be able to laugh.[3]

Think carefully about this quote. It says something very significant about building a life filled with love.

And so we come to the end of *Dare to Connect*. And to you who are reading this book at this very moment, I say the same thing that was said to me those many years ago: "I don't know your name; but I know who you are." And . . .

Who you are is someone who has the power within to create a Heaven on earth for yourself and to radiate a piece of that Heaven out to everyone whose life touches yours.

There will be times when you forget this important truth. So to help you imprint it **permanently** in your mind, I'd like you to write the following sentence on a little card, carry it with you wherever you go, and read it at least ten times every single day of your life from this day forth:

"Who I am is someone who has the power within to create a Heaven on earth for myself and to radiate a piece of that Heaven out to everyone whose life touches mine."

Say it out loud now. Say it again. Say it yet again. Feel the bliss inherent in such an awesomely powerful message. Repeat it over and over again for as many days, months, or years as it takes, until you **fully** feel it, hear it, breathe it, see it, walk it, and talk it . . . that is, until you fully take in its implications and begin consciously to live your life within its truth. In that you will find an unending surge of joy, light, and love that will nourish and support you all the days of your life.

APPENDIX

A Guided Visualization for Connecting with Confidence

A guided visualization is a powerful way to tap into the parts of your being that are usually clouded by the negative mind. It is designed to help you get in touch with your Higher Self—the part of you that is loving, creative, intuitive, joyful, giving, abundant, the part of you that knows **there is nothing to fear.**

A guided visualization is most effective on audiotape; therefore, I suggest you softly, gently, and **very** slowly speak the following into a tape recorder. If you find your own voice too distracting, ask a friend to speak it into a tape recorder for you. I've provided dotted lines to indicate where there should be silence on the tape to allow time for the instructions to be followed. (A good tip is to speak more slowly and leave more time for the instructions then you think are necessary.)*

*I've recorded a similar visualization on Tape 2, Side 2, of a workshop entitled FLIRTING FROM THE HEART. (Hay House, 1154 E. Dominguez, P.O. Box 6204, Carson, CA 90749-6204, 800-654-5126, 1987.)

You need to set the stage. Select a time when you are unlikely to be disturbed. You may even want to take the telephone off the hook. Find yourself a comfortable position, either lying down or sitting in a chair with your spine straight, both feet on the floor and hands in your lap.

As you listen to the instructions, **don't try to monitor the thoughts or pictures that come into your head,** even if they seem silly. Some of you may not see anything at all. Not to worry. Visualizations are very effective for some, but not for everyone. Relax, knowing there are many other ways to access the Higher Self, such as the use of affirmations or meditation. Also, don't be upset if you get a negative picture. Sometimes negative pictures tell us as much as positive ones. Just look for the message that is being given to you and make it a learning experience. You may find yourself dozing off. That's OK, too. Just try again another day.

The following is a guided visualization designed to allow you greater ease in connecting with yourself and everyone around you. It is meant to enhance your feeling of power and love and to help you step comfortably into any type of social situation. Here are the words for your tape recorder:

Find yourself a comfortable position and close your eyes . . .

Take a very deep breath . . . and then let go. . . .

Once again, take another deep breath and feel the energy coursing throughout your body . . . and let go. . . .

Take another deep breath, this time imagining yourself breathing in the loving light of the Universe . . . and as you release, see yourself breathing out loving light into the Universe. . . .

Enjoy the peace of just being there . . . having nothing to do but to listen to these words. Ignore the sounds around you as well as the unrelated thoughts that come into your head. . . . Allow what you feel for you to come up.

Begin to relax your body . . . from the top of your head to the tips of your toes . . . relax . . . between your eyes . . . relax . . . Relax your cheeks . . . your jaw . . . your neck . . . your shoulders . . . arms . . . relax. . . .

Take another deep breath and feel yourself relaxing all over . . . your chest . . . your back . . . stomach . . . thighs . . . calves . . . ankles . . . feet . . . Let it all go. . . .

Take one more deep breath and if you are still holding tension in any area of your body, just let go. . . .

Now . . . in your mind's eye, imagine yourself getting ready to go to some social event. . . . It could be a party, a meeting, a class or whatever your mind envisions. . . .

See yourself dressing for the occasion . . . and as you look into the mirror, see a beautiful and confident you, the *you* you always wanted to be. Smile as you get a sense, not of your physical beauty, but of the richness and warmth that you hold inside. . . .

As you look into the mirror, you are instilled with a wonderful sense of confidence. You feel your own power, your own ability to love, and you know that you have something to offer everyone you meet. . . . Really get into those feelings of power, confidence and love. . . .

And as you stand in front of that mirror, affirm to yourself. . . .

"I am a powerful and loving person and I have much to give. I am creating light wherever I go."

Really experience the power in those words. . . .

Stand tall . . . and look into your eyes, seeing only the beauty that lies within . . . the part of you that is loving, giving, and caring. Breathe in those feelings, knowing this part of you really exists. . . .

Take a moment to enjoy that beautiful image in the mirror. . . .

Now transport yourself to the door of this special event and look inside. . . . See all the assembled guests . . . and, as you stand there, once again allow yourself to feel your own magnificence. . . .

This time affirm to yourself,

"I am a beautiful person. My purpose here today is to make others feel good about who they are. . . ."

Allow yourself to feel confident, self-assured, caring and loving, knowing that you have your own special contribution to bring to the people in the room. . . . Let yourself experience the power and love that comes from that knowledge. . . .

Standing tall and confident, step inside knowing that you are a very valuable member of this group . . . and begin interacting with the people in the room. . . .

Feel what it would feel like to have no fear of rejection, no self-consciousness, only focusing outward to the people in the room. . . .

With this sense of confidence, what would you be doing? . . . See yourself making others feel at ease, knowing they are probably nervous and insecure. . . . See yourself interested, caring, and sensitive to their insecurities. . . . What would you be doing? Really look at yourself. . . .

Look at the love in your own heart. . . . Realize that everybody in the room wants to connect. They want to feel loved and accepted . . . just like you. Remember, there truly are no strangers. . . .

Just knowing you have so much to give takes away the fear. . . . You feel comfortable . . . flowing. . . . See yourself interacting . . . giving . . . asking . . . loving . . . listening . . . caring. . . .

Now look around. . . . How would others be reacting to you when you are confident and loving? . . . What would they be doing? . . . See them interacting with you. . . . What does it look like? . . . What would you be doing now, caring about others, being interested in others? . . . Watch yourself . . . and watch how others are reacting to you. . . .

See yourself the way you'd like to be. . . . and know that you can create this picture in reality. . . . Slowly, you can build your confidence. . . . You can train your mind to see your true nature . . . the loving person that you are . . .

Enjoy being in this room for a few more seconds. . . . Look at the love around you. . . . Look at the love in your own heart. . . . Realize that everyone in the room wants to connect. . . . They want to feel whole. . . . They want to feel love just as you do . . . and you have the capacity to contribute to their lives. . . .

Bathe in the feeling of belonging for just a few moments. . . .

And when you are ready, start to bring yourself back into the room. . . . Be aware of your body . . .

Start to move around and stretch. . . .

Take a deep breath knowing that you can return to this place within any time you wish. . . . And when you are ready, open your eyes.

And as you "come back" from this healing and peaceful way of being, it would be helpful to write down any observations you might have had which may be of future value to you. If you feel you learned from this visualization, repeat it frequently. Do it before any social gathering. It will bolster your self-confidence enormously and remind you of how much love you have to give to this world.

Chapter Notes

CHAPTER 1

1. Ram Dass, *Who Are You?* (Arlington, VA: The Soundworks, Inc.) (Audiotape).

2. John Bradshaw, *Healing the Shame That Binds You* (Deerfield Beach, FL: Health Communications, Inc., 1988) p. vii.

3. John Powell, *Why Am I Afraid to Tell You Who I Am* (Allen, TX: Argus Communications, 1969) p. 134.

CHAPTER 3

1. Alan Cohen, *Rising in Love: The Journey into Light* (South Kortright, NY: Eden Company, 1983) p. 143.

2. Powell, *Why Am I Afraid to Tell You Who I Am,* p. 12.

3. Many additional self-esteem exercises can be found in my earlier books *Feel the Fear and Do It Anyway* (New York: Fawcett Columbine, 1987) and *Opening Our Hearts to Men* (Fawcett Columbine, 1989). Men, the exercises in *Opening Our Hearts to Men* will work for you as well!

4. Linda Weltner, "The Miracle of Imperfection," *New Age Journal* (September/October 1990) p. 136.

5. Three audiotapes I created for daily use are *Inner Talk for Peace*

of Mind, Inner Talk for a Confident Day, and *Inner Talk for a Love That Works.* (Hay House, P.O. Box 6204 Dept. SJ, Carson, CA 90749-6204, (800) 654-5126).

6. Louise L. Hay, *The AIDS Book: Creating a Positive Approach* (Carson, CA: Hay House, 1988) p. 114. While this book focuses on AIDS, it is relevant to all of us, as it is primarily a book about self-love.

7. W. W. Broadbent, *How to Be Loved* (New York: Warner Books, 1976.) pp. 28–43.

8. Bradshaw, *Healing the Shame That Binds You,* p. 14.

9. The Twelve-Step programs are based on a philosophy of life which helps you understand, discover, and use your spiritual nature. For information about CODA in your area write to: Co-dependents Anonymous, Inc., P.O. Box 33577, Phoenix, AZ 85067-3577, or phone (602) 277-7991.

10. Two books that describe the process of inner-child work are *Healing Your Aloneness: Finding Love and Wholeness through Your Inner Child,* by Erika Chopich and Margaret Paul (San Francisco: Harper & Row, 1990) and *Homecoming: Reclaiming and Championing Your Inner Child* by John Bradshaw (New York: Bantam Books, 1990).

CHAPTER 4

1. Ira Tanner, *Loneliness: The Fear of Love* (New York: Harper & Row, 1973) p. 48.

2. Anne Morrow Lindbergh, *Gift from the Sea* (New York: Pantheon Books, 1955) p. 42.

3. Henri J. M. Nouwen, *Out of Solitude* (Notre Dame: Ave Marie Press, 1974) p. 22.

4. Chapters of The Inside Edge can be found in Los Angeles, Orange County, and San Diego. For information write: The Inside Edge, P.O. Box 692, Pacific Palisades, CA 90272, or phone (213)-649-1442.

CHAPTER 5

1. "Imaginary" healing light can be used in many ways: to soothe diseased parts of the body, to make you feel more peaceful, to create more harmony in your life, and to help you reach out to others. You might want to investigate further. Sanaya Roman includes a chapter entitled "Creating with Light" in her book *Spiritual Growth* (Tiburon, CA: H. J. Kramer, Inc.)

2. Stuart Wilde, *Affirmations* (Taos, NM: White Dove International, 1987) p. 37.

3. Dale Carnegie, *How to Win Friends and Influence People* (New York: Pocket Books, 1936) p. 66.

4. Jack Canfield, *Self-Esteem: Your Key to Success* (Culver City, CA). (Audiotape)

5. Hay, *The AIDS Book: Creating a Positive Approach,* p. 256.

6. Ralph Waldo Trine, *In Tune with the Infinite* (London: Unwin Paperbacks, 1965) p. 2.

CHAPTER 6

1. Antoine de Saint-Éxupery, *The Little Prince* (Troy, MO: Harcourt Brace Jovanovich, 1943) p. 70.

2. Susan Jeffers, *Feel the Fear and Do It Anyway* (New York: Fawcett Columbine, 1987) pp. 135–149.

3. David Burns, *Intimate Connections* (New York: New American Library, 1985) p. xvi.

4. Jeffers, *Opening Our Hearts to Men,* p. 57.

CHAPTER 7

1. Sam Keen, *The Passionate Life: Stages of Loving* (San Francisco: Harper & Row, 1983) pp. 216–217.

2. Richard (Coyote) Prosapio in Valentine Riddell's, "The Men's Movement," *Sante Fe Spirit* magazine (August/September 1990) p. 22.

3. *The Twelve Steps: A Way Out* (San Diego: Recovery Publications, Inc., 1987).

CHAPTER 8

1. Ken Druck with James C. Simmons, *The Secrets Men Keep: Breaking the Silence Barrier* (Garden City, NY: Doubleday and Company, Inc., 1985) p. 144.

2. Keen, *The Passionate Life: Stages of Loving*, p. 121.

3. Michael E. McGill, *The McGill Report on Male Intimacy* (New York: Harper & Row, 1985) p. 173.

4. In *Opening Our Hearts to Men*, I discuss our lagging expectations and ways we can catch up more quickly (pp. 71–96). Men, this is for you as well.

5. George Blooston, "Is There a Wild Man in Your Life," *New Woman* (July 1990) p. 77.

6. Ibid., p. 74.

7. Alan Cohen, *Rising in Love: The Journey into Light*, p. 126.

CHAPTER 9

1. Ram Dass, *Beyond Success* (Delray Beach, FL: Hanuman Tape Library, 1989), from a workshop entitled "On Work, Money and Burnout." (Audiotape)

2. Charles Simpkinson, "Seeking the Soul of Capitalism," *Common Boundary* magazine, 8528 Bradford Road, Silver Springs, MD 20901 (July/August 1990) p. 31.

3. Donald Marrs, *Executive in Passage* (Los Angeles: Barrington Sky Publishing, 1990), p. 244.

4. Jeffers, *Feel the Fear and Do It Anyway*, pp. 189–204.

5. To learn more about Aikido, read Thomas Crum, *The Magic of Conflict* (New York: Simon and Schuster, 1987) and Tim Piering, *Mastery: A Technology for Excellence and Personal Evolution* (Sierra Madre, CA: Sun West Publishing Co., 1988).

6. Alfie Kohn, *No Contest: The Case Against Competition* (Boston: Houghton Mifflin Co., 1986).

7. Alfie, Kohn, "The Case Against Competition," Noetic Sciences Review, Institute of Noetic Sciences: 475 Gate 5 Road, Suite 300, Sausalito, CA 94965, (415)331-5650. (Spring 1990) p. 18.

8. Riane Eisler, *The Chalice and the Blade* (San Francisco: Harper & Row, 1987) p. xvii.

9. Merle Shain, *Hearts That We Broke Long Ago* (New York: Bantam Books, 1985) p. 71.

10. Sally Helgesen, *The Female Advantage: Women's Ways of Leadership* New York: Doubleday, 1990)

11. Ibid., p. 5.

12. Ibid., p. 144.

13. Simpkinson, "Seeking the Soul of Capitalism," p. 31–33.

CHAPTER 10

1. "A Course in Miracles" is a self-study program of spiritual healing. (Foundation for Inner Peace) Marianne Williamson is one of its teachers.

2. Marianne Williamson, *Cosmic Adulthood* (Los Angeles: Miracle Projects). (Audiotape)

3. Harold Kushner, *When All You've Ever Wanted Isn't Enough* (New York: Summit Books, 1986) pp. 165–166.

Resources:
Books and Audiotapes*

Abbott, Franklin, ed. *New Men, New Minds: Breaking Male Tradition.* Freedom, CA: The Crossing Press, 1987.

Bloomfield, Harold, *Making Peace with Yourself: Turning Your Weaknesses into Strengths.* New York: Ballantine Books, 1990.

Bradshaw, John. *Healing the Shame That Binds You.* Health Communications, Inc.: Enterprise Center, 3201 S.W. 15th St., Deerfield Beach, FL 33442, 1988.

Bradshaw, John. *Homecoming: Reclaiming Your Inner Child.* New York: Bantam Books, 1990.

Broadbent, W. W. *How to Be Loved.* New York: Warner Books, 1976.

Burns, David D. *Intimate Connections.* New York: New American Library, 1985.

Canfield, Jack. *Self-Esteem: Your Key to Success.* 6035 Bristol Parkway, Culver City, CA 90230. (Audiotape)

Carnegie, Dale. *How to Win Friends and Influence People.* New York: Pocket Books, 1936.

Chopich, Erika J., and Paul, Margaret. *Healing Your Aloneness: Finding Love and Wholeness through Your Inner Child.* San Francisco: Harper & Row, 1990.

*If you can't find a book or tape on the shelves, ask the salesperson to order it for you. Sometimes books and audiotapes go out of print and are simply not available in stores. They may be found in the library.

Cohen, Alan. *Rising in Love: The Journey into Light*. Eden Company, South Kortright, NY, in cooperation with Coleman Graphics: 99 Milbar Blvd., Farmingdale, NY 11735, 1983.

Crum, Thomas. *The Magic of Conflict*. New York: Simon & Schuster, Inc., 1987.

Druck, Ken, with Simmons, James C. *The Secrets Men Keep*. New Garden City, NY: Doubleday and Company, Inc., 1985.

Dyer, Wayne, *Your Erroneous Zones: Step-by-Step Advice for Escaping the Trap of Negative Thinking & Take Control of Your Life*. New York: Harper Collins, 1991.

Eichberg, Rob. *Coming Out: An Act of Love*. New York: Dutton, 1990.

Eisler, Riane. *The Chalice and the Blade*. San Francisco: Harper & Row, 1987.

Eisler, Riane, and Loye, David. *The Partnership Way: New Tools for Learning and Living*. New York: Harper & Row, 1990.

Farrell, Warren. *Why Men Are the Way They Are*. New York: McGraw Hill, 1986.

Forward, Susan, *Obsessive Love*. New York: Bantam Books, 1991.

Foundation for Inner Peace. *A Course in Miracles*. P.O. Box 635 Tiburon, CA 94920: 1975.

Hay, Louise. *The AIDS Book: Creating a Positive Approach*. Hay House: P.O. Box 6204, Carson, CA 90749-6204, 1988.

Helgesen, Sally. *The Female Advantage: Women's Ways of Leadership*. New York: Doubleday, 1990.

Huang, Al Chung-liang. *Embrace Tiger, Return to Mountain: The Essence of T'ai Chi*. Real People Press: Box F, Moab, UT, 84532, 1973.

Jeffers, Susan. *The Art of Fearbusting*. Hay House: P.O. Box 6204, Dept. SJ, Carson, CA 90749-6204, (800)654-5126, 1986 (Audiotape)

Jeffers, Susan. *Dare to Connect: Reaching Out in Romance, Friendship and the Workplace*. Hay House, 1992 (Audiotape)

Jeffers, Susan. *A Fearbusting Workshop*. Hay House, 1987. (Audiotape)

Jeffers, Susan. *"The Fear-Less Series": Inner Talk for Peace of Mind; Inner Talk for a Confident Day, Inner Talk for a Love That Works*. Hay House, 1990. (Affirmation Audiotapes)

Jeffers, Susan. *Feel the Fear and Do It Anyway*. New York: Fawcett Columbine, 1987.

Jeffers, Susan. *Feel the Fear and Do It Anyway*. Nightingale Conant Audio: 7300 North Lehigh Avenue, Chicago, IL 60648, (800) 572-2770, 1988. (Booktape)

Jeffers, Susan. *Flirting from the Heart*. Hay House, 1987. (Audiotape)

Jeffers, Susan. *The Journey from Lost to Found*. New York: Fawcett Columbine, 1993.

Jeffers, Susan. *Opening Our Hearts to Men*. New York: Fawcett Columbine, 1989.

Jeffers, Susan. *Opening Our Hearts to Each Other*. Hay House, 1989. (Audiotape)

Jeffers, Susan. *Opening Our Hearts to Men*. Hay House, 1989. (Booktape)

Keen, Sam. *The Passionate Life: Stages of Loving*. San Francisco: Harper & Row, 1983.

Kohn, Alfie. *No Contest: The Case Against Competition*. Boston: Houghton Mifflin Co., 1986.

Kushner, Harold. *When All You've Ever Wanted Isn't Enough*. New York: Summit Books, 1986.

Lindbergh, Anne Morrow. *Gift from the Sea*. New York: Pantheon Books, 1955.

Louise, Diana. *Journey into New Dimensions: A Beginner's Meditation and Visualization Tape*. 270 N. Canon Dr., Ste. 1309, Y.O.G.A. Productions: Beverly Hills, CA 90210. (Audiotape)

Lozoff, Bo. *We're All Doing Time*. Rte 1, Box 201N, Durham, NC 27705: Human Kindness Foundation, 1985.

Marrs, Donald. *Executive in Passage*. Barrington Sky Publishing: P.O. Box 49428, Los Angeles, CA 90049, 1990.

Marston, Stephanie. *The Magic of Encouragement: Nurturing Your Child's Self-Esteem*. New York: William Morrow & Company, 1990.

May, Rollo. *Man's Search for Himself*. New York: Dell Publishing, 1953.

McGill, Michael E. *The McGill Report on Male Intimacy*. New York: Harper & Row, 1985.

Nouwen, J. M. *Out of Solitude*. Notre Dame, IN: Ave Maria Press, 1974.

Piering, Tim. *Mastery: A Technology for Excellence and Personal Evolution*. Sun West Publishing Co.: 370 W. Sierra Madre Blvd., F, Sierra Madre, CA 91024, 1988.

Powell, John. *Why Am I Afraid to Tell You Who I Am*. Argus Communications: One DLM Park, Allen, TX 75002, 1969.

Ram Dass, *Who Are You?* The Soundworks, Inc: 911 N. Fillmore St., Arlington, VA 22201. (Audiotape)

Ram Dass. *Beyond Success*. Hanuman Tape Library: P.O. Box 2320, Delray Beach, FL 33447, 1989. (Audiotape)

Ram Dass, and Gorman, Paul. *How Can I Help?* New York: Alfred A. Knopf, 1987.

Roman, Sanaya. *Spiritual Growth*. H. J. Kramer, Inc.: P.O. Box 1082, Tiburon, CA 94920.

de Saint-Éxupery, Antoine. *The Little Prince*. Troy, MO: Harcourt Brace Jovanovich, 1943.

Shain, Merle. *Hearts That We Broke Long Ago*. New York: Bantam Books, 1985.

Stone, Hal, and Winkelman, Sidra. *Embracing Our Selves: Voice Dialogue Manual*. Devorss & Company: P.O. Box 550, Marina del Rey, CA 90294, 1985.

Storr, Anthony. *Solitude: A Return to the Self*. New York, Ballantine Books, 1988.

Tanner, Ira. *Loneliness: The Fear of Love*. New York: Harper & Row, 1973.

Trine, Ralph Waldo. *In Tune with the Infinite*. 15–17 Broadwick Street, London WIV IFP: Unwin Paperbacks, 1965.

The Twelve Steps: A Way Out. Recovery Publications: 1201 Knoxville St., San Diego, CA 92110, 1987.

Wilde, Stuart. *Affirmations*. White Dove International: P.O. Box 1000, Taos, NM 87571, 1987.

Williamson, Marianne. *Cosmic Adulthood*. Miracle Projects: 1550 N. Hayworth Ave., #1, Los Angeles CA 90046. (Audiotape)

About the Author

SUSAN JEFFERS, Ph.D., is a noted public speaker, workshop leader, and media personality. She has created numerous audiotapes on the subjects of fear, relationships, and personal growth and is the author of *Feel the Fear and Do It Anyway, Opening Our Hearts to Men, Dare to Connect, The Journey from Lost to Found,* and the "Fear-Less" series of affirmation books *(Inner Talk for a Love That Works, Inner Talk for Peace of Mind,* and *Inner Talk for a Confident Day)*. Dr. Jeffers lives with her husband in New Mexico.